New Zealand Bird Views

OYSTERCATCHERS

Raewyn Adams

Published 2013
Te Puke, New Zealand.
© Text and photos Raewyn Adams
The author asserts her moral right to be identified as the author of this work.

ISBN 978-0-473-23960-2

Copies of this book can be purchased from www.lulu.com
Author contact radams.photo@gmail.com

Front cover: Black morph variable oystercatcher at Mount Maunganui.

CONTENTS

SERIES INTRODUCTION

The concept of this series is to present and appreciate the birds that people are likely to view around them. These are the common birds that are around us every day but we fail to really see because they are always just "there".

The intent of this series is to tell the bird's story in photos. In this format the reader can see more of the bird's life and gain an understanding and appreciation of its place in nature and how it interacts with the world it lives in – its relationships with other birds, the environment and also with people.

When you get to know them, birds are fascinating animals. They have complex social structures, sophisticated communication systems and are very hard workers. They are also very beautiful. The feathers of even the plainest birds have amazing textures and intricate patterns.

I have provided some basic factual information. For those wanting more depth there is a starting point in the list of further information resources at the end of the book. The rest of the book consists of my personal observations, illustrated with photographs as much as possible.

I hope you enjoy these views of the birds around us.

OYSTERCATCHERS IN NEW ZEALAND

Two species of oystercatcher are commonly seen in New Zealand:

- **South Island pied oystercatcher** (*Haematopus finschi)* Also known as SIPO. Breeds only in inland South Island areas then migrates to the coast in winter. There are believed to be over 100,000 birds. Size 460mm. Endemic, which means found only in New Zealand.

- **Variable oystercatcher** (*Haematopus unicolor)*. Also known as VOC. This bird lives and breeds on the coast. There are about 4000 birds. Size 470-490mm. Endemic

These two species of oystercatcher are the only two likely to be seen in mainland New Zealand. *Haematopus chathamensis* is a third New Zealand oystercatcher species but as the name suggests, it comes from the Chatham Islands and is found only there.

SIPOs and VOCs have quite distinct habitats, but are also frequently seen close together because the SIPOs disperse to the coast after breeding and can be found at the same locations as VOCs.

Oystercatchers are easily recognised by their distinct black or pied colour, their large red bill and their stocky body shape. There is no other bird at all similar to an all-black variable oystercatcher.

Pied oystercatchers are larger than pied stilts, have a much different feeding habit from pied shags and are

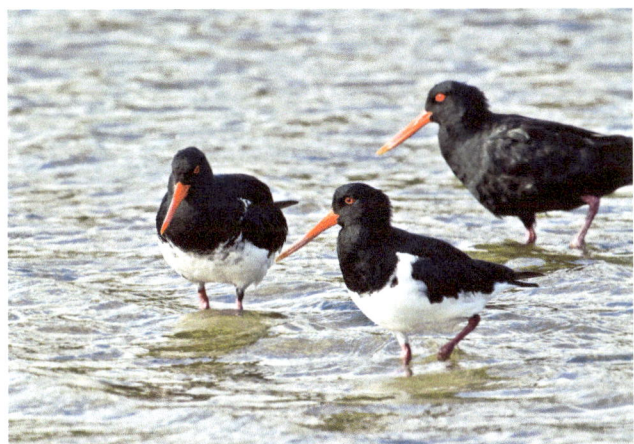

South Island pied oystercatcher in front. Pied morph variable oystercatcher at left. Black morph variable oystercatcher in the background. Ruakaka, Northland. April.

much stockier in appearance than both of these so are unlikely to be confused with either. Although these birds share the pied colouration, only the oystercatcher has the large red bill.

When seen together at estuaries, both species of oystercatcher will feed near each other as they wade in shallow water seeking the shellfish and worms that comprise the majority of their diet.

At high tide they usually roost in flocks waiting for low tide to expose their food again. These flocks may be a mix of both species, often on sand bars or shell banks. A single flock may show a loose species division, with some mixing at the point of overlap. When there are large numbers of both species they are more likely to maintain separate flocks.

The life span is up tp 25 years for SIPOs and possibly up to 30 years for VOCs.

SOUTH ISLAND PIED OYSTERCATCHER

Flocks of South Island pied oystercatchers (SIPOs) can be recognised by their uniform appearance that includes a distinct white shoulder patch. The demarcation between black and white on the chest is a clean line and all birds in the flock look very similar to one another. There is very little variation between individuals.

The wing shows a clear cut broad white band. This can be seen next to the white under-body when the bird is at rest and is also visible in flight, giving an appearance of black and white striped wings. This pattern is the same in all SIPOs.

The general appearance of the SIPO is of a slightly smaller and slimmer bird than the variable oystercatcher (VOC). Also, in the SIPO the bill is slightly thinner and more pointed than that of the VOC which is thicker with a more round end.

From August to January SIPOs breed in the riverbeds and farmland of the South Island. They are located from Marlborough to Southland, mainly to the east of the main divide. They pair up to the same pairs as the previous season, although the individuals may have wintered in different places.

After breeding has finished for the year the birds migrate to northern harbours, estuaries and coastal locations with individuals usually returning to the same wintering ground each year. Flocks can consist of several thousand birds in places such as Kaipara and Manukau Harbours and at Miranda. Smaller flocks can also be seen at many other locations.

Those birds that remain in the South Island over winter usually migrate to the Nelson area. Non-breeding (often young) birds may stay at the coast year round.

During the breeding season when the birds are inland, insects, invertebrates and earthworms are the main food eaten. When residing at coastal locations, the diet consists of marine crustaceans, molluscs, bivalves, marine worms and possibly small fish.

Very similar to the widespread Eurasian or Common pied oystercatcher *Haematopus ostralegus,* the SIPO is sometimes considered to be a sub-species of this but is now generally accepted as being a separate species.

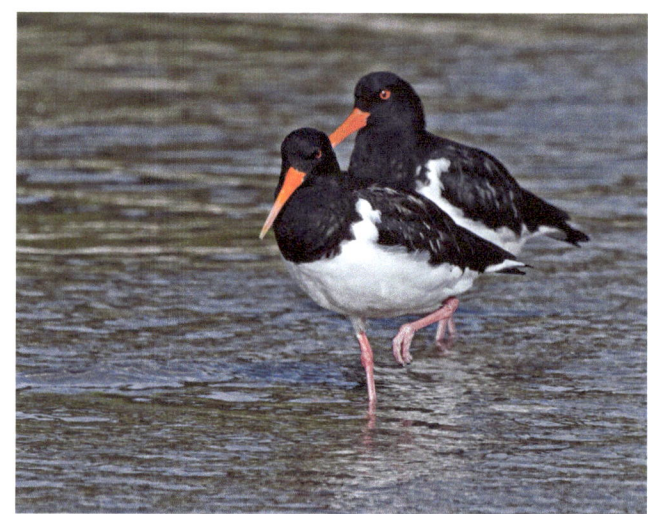

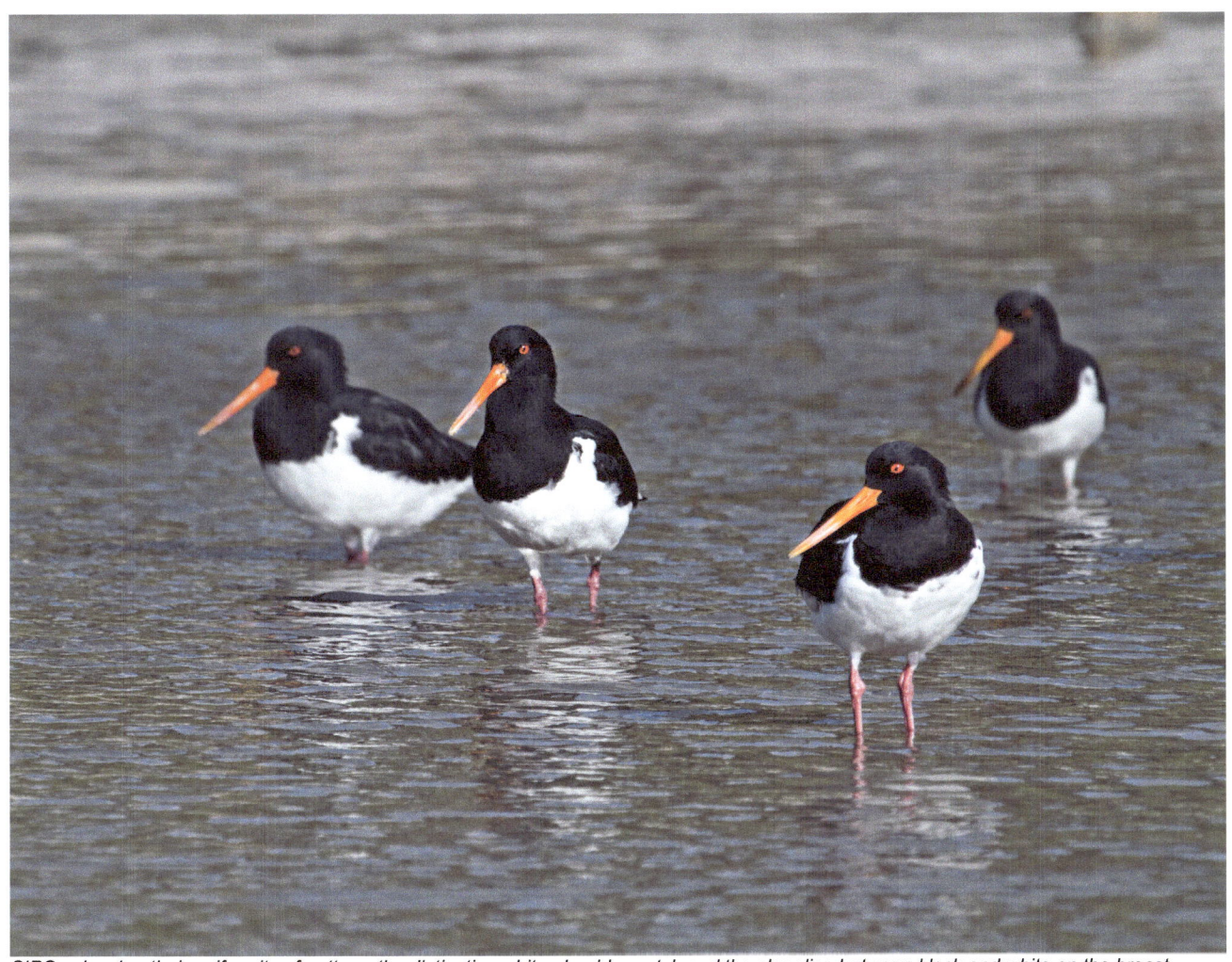

SIPOs showing their uniformity of pattern, the distinctive white shoulder patch and the clear line between black and white on the breast. Above and left Ruakaka. April.

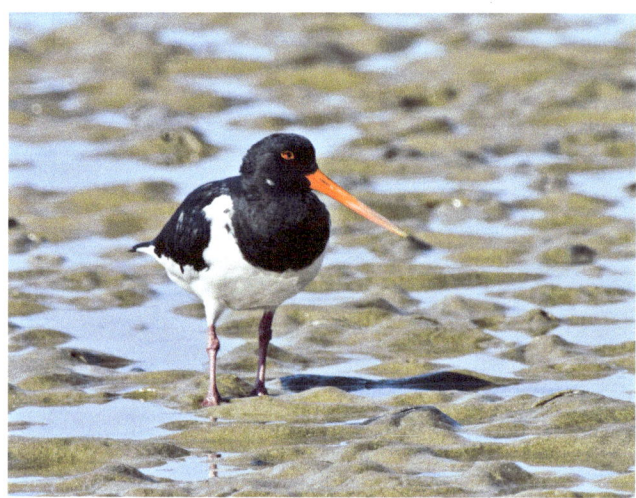

Ruakaka, Northland. April.

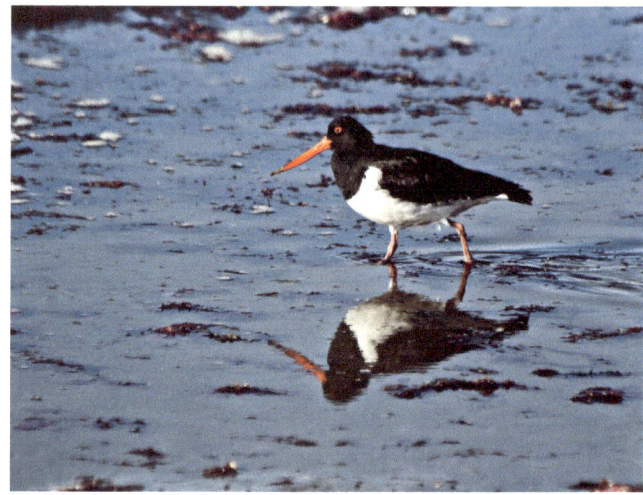

Marfell's Beach, Marlborough. March.

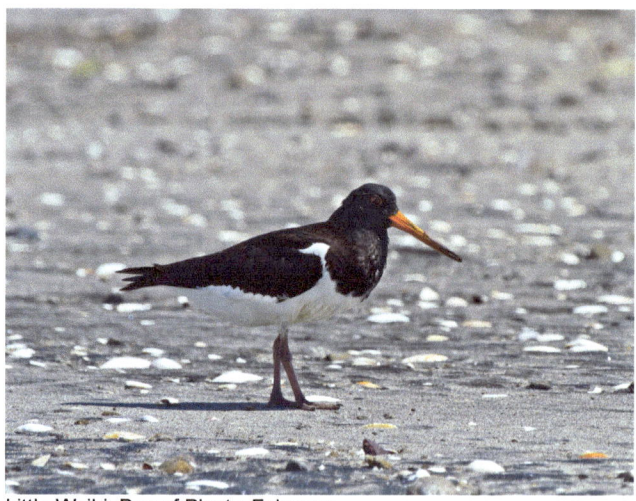

Little Waihi, Bay of Plenty. February.

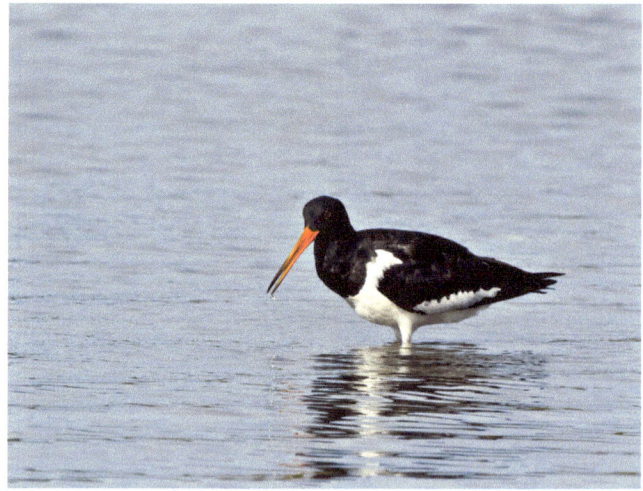

Little Waihi, Bay of Plenty. February.

4

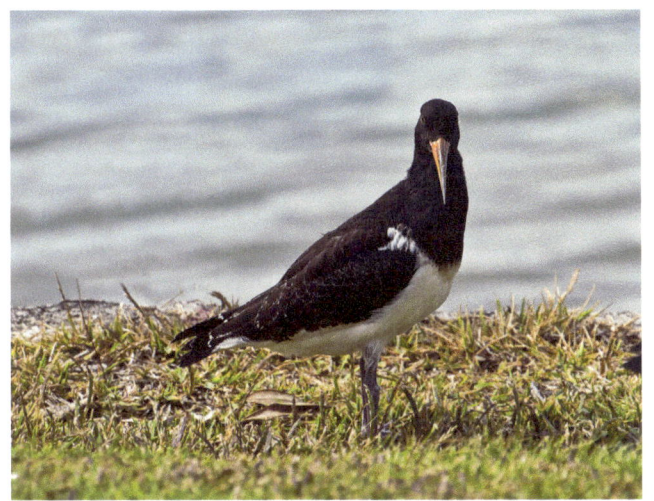

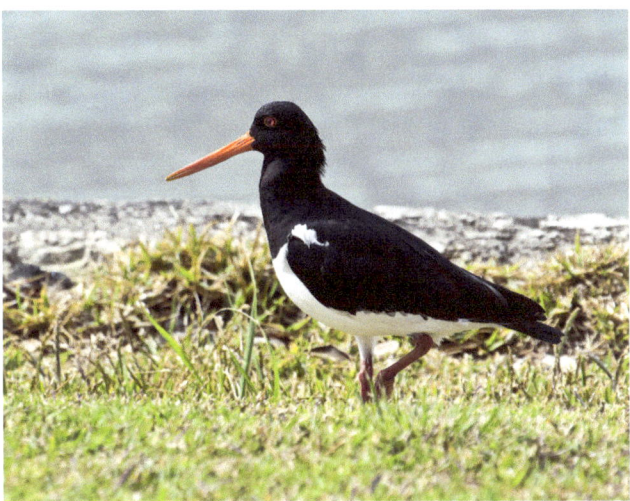

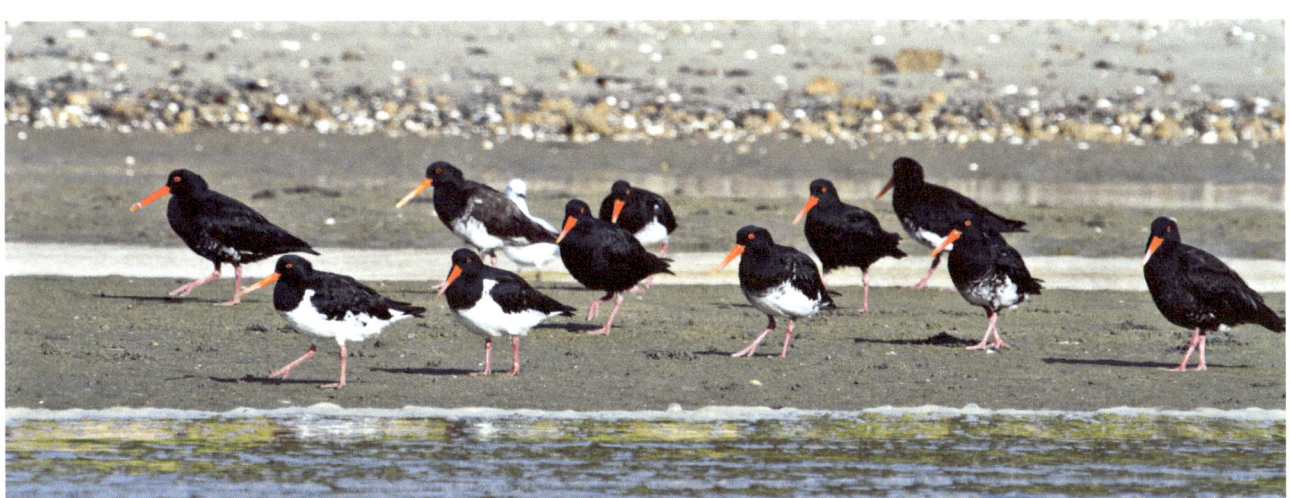

The colour of the immature SIPO at top left is dull compared to the adult at top right. The adult is a bright black with bright red bill and distinctly pink legs. Above - Two SIPOs at front left The other birds are all VOCs showing the degree of pattern variation that occurs. The high proportion of pied morph VOCs is typical of Northland. All Ruakaka, Northland. April.

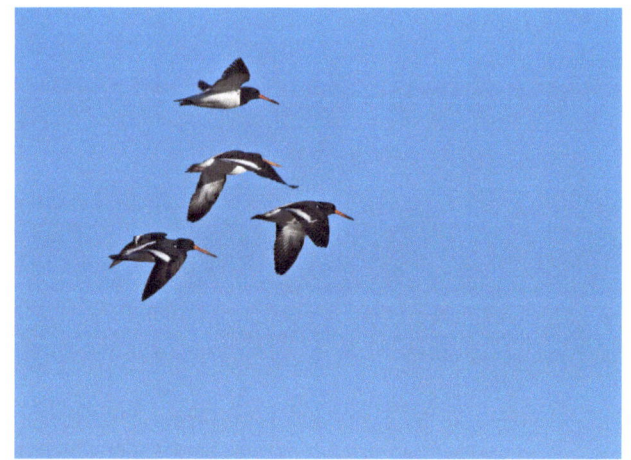

Ruakaka, Northland. April.

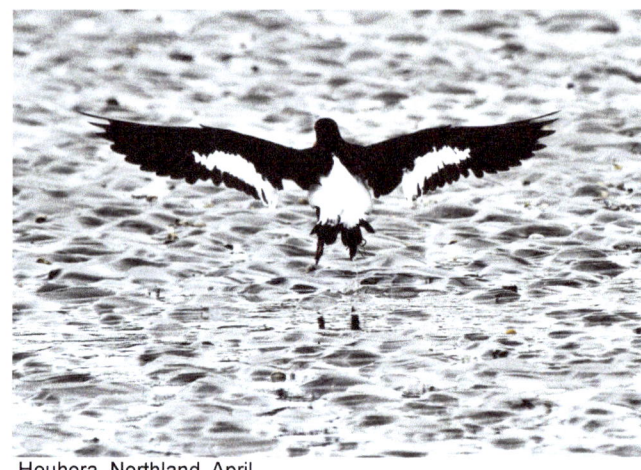

Houhora, Northland. April.

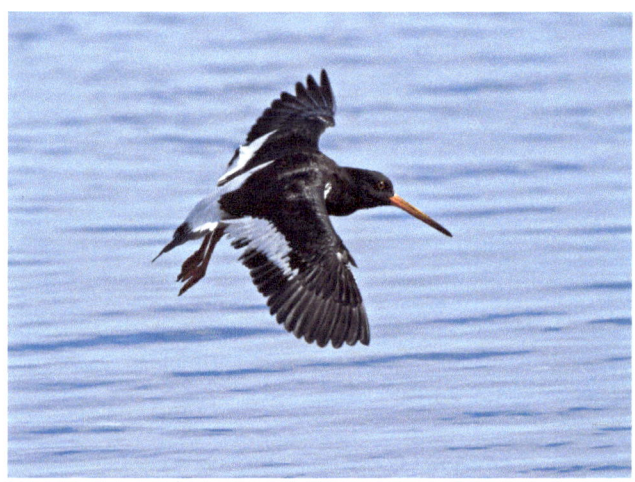

Little Waihi, Bay of Plenty. February.

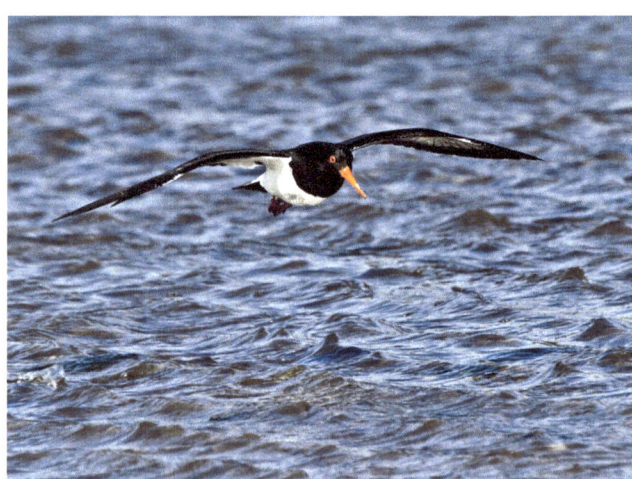

Maketu, Bay of plenty. April.

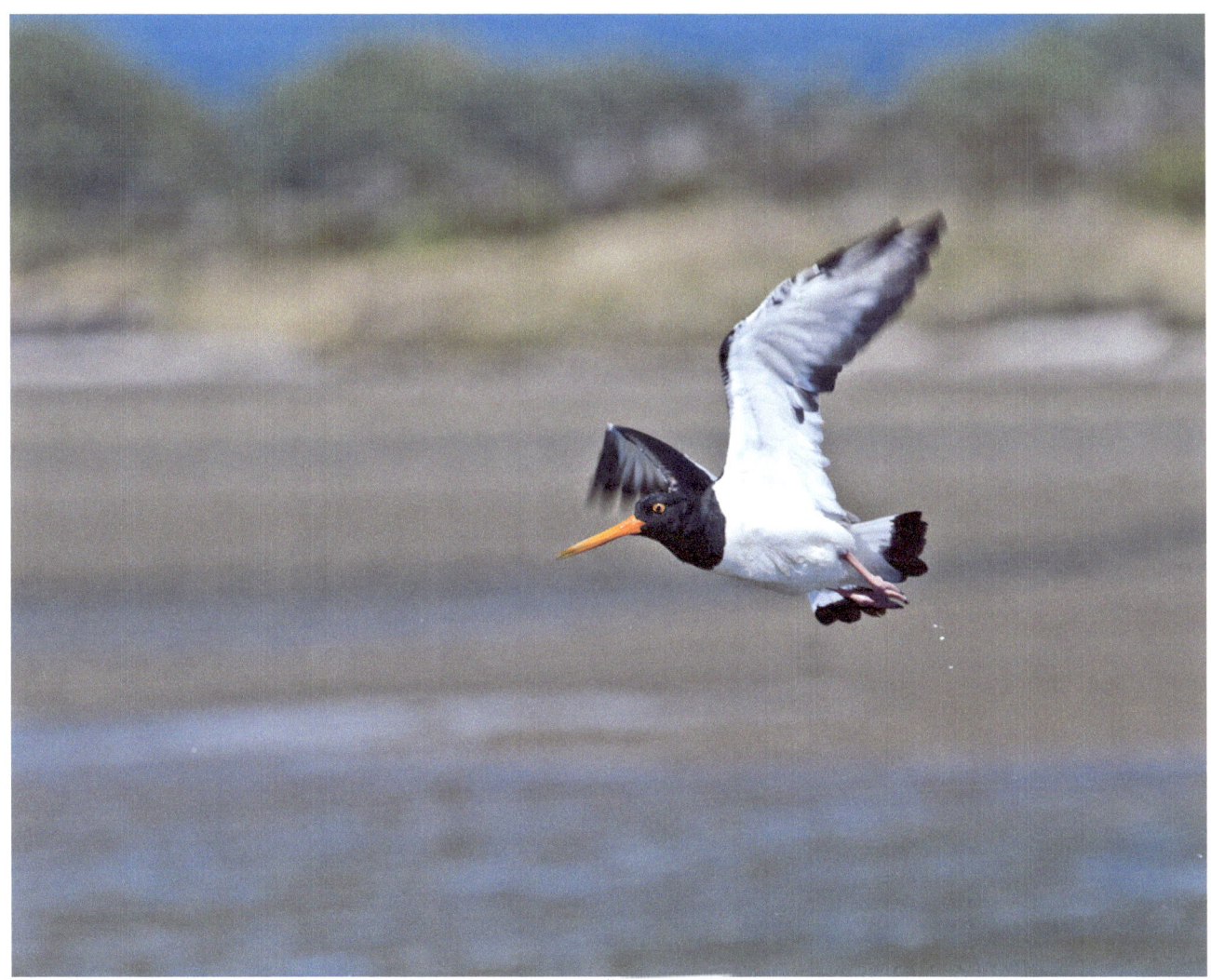

Above and opposite - views of SIPOs in flight. The distinctive wing patterns can be seen, as well as the clear line between black and white on the breast (Above). Little Waihi, Bay of Plenty. February.

VARIABLE OYSTERCATCHER

The variable oystercatcher (VOC) is named for its variable colouration. Birds can be found in three colour morphs: black, pied and intermediate. These colour variations (also called phases) are permanent. Whatever morph the bird is, it stays that colour for life.

In the black morph, the birds are all black with no white feathers at all, although feathers may fade to dark brown as they wear. Black morph birds may be seen throughout New Zealand but are more common in the south to the extent that in the far south and Stewart Island usually only black birds are seen.

The pied morph VOC can look similar to the South Island pied oystercatcher (SIPO). It is mainly seen in the northern North Island, especially in Northland, and can be distinguished from the SIPO by its slightly larger size with heavier bill, and by the less clean line between black and white on the chest. The shoulder patch that is clear cut in the SIPO is usually missing, or if present will be less distinct on the pied morph VOC.

In between these two distinct colour morphs is the intermediate morph which is a bird that has some white feathers on its underside, but not as much white as the pied morph VOC. These birds appear wherever there are mixed populations of pied and black morph VOCs. Around the central North Island coasts about 85% of the birds will be all black and the rest a mix of pied and intermediate morph. In the far north slightly more than half the birds seen will have some white markings.

VOCs remain near the coast throughout the year. They are most abundant on the north eastern coast of the North Island from the Far North to Hawkes Bay and also in the Wellington region. In the South Island they are most common in northern regions and Fiordland.

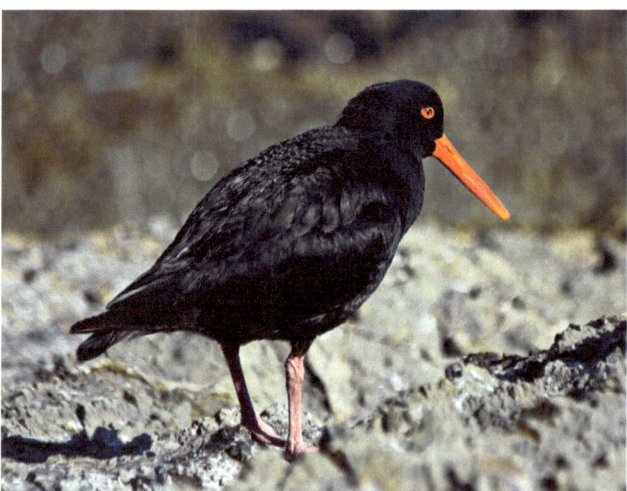

Black morph VOC showing a bright black glossy sheen. Whakatane, Bay of Plenty. February.

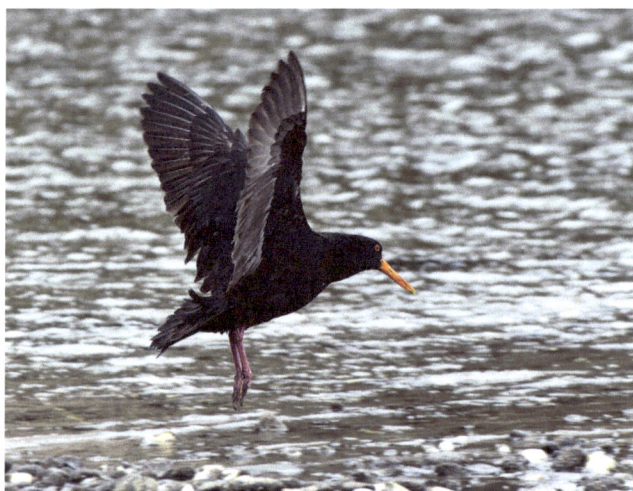

Black VOC coming into land showing the different shades of black and brown in its wings. Pukehina, Bay of Plenty. February.

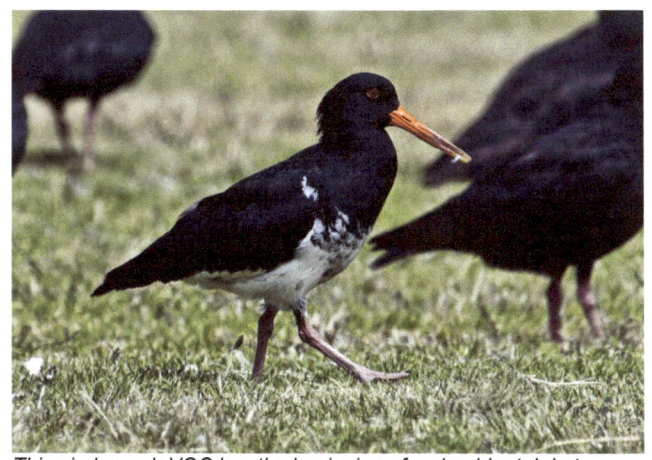

This pied morph VOC has the beginning of a shoulder tab but overall the white area is mottled with black instead of being clean as in SIPO. Little Waihi, Bay of Plenty. January.

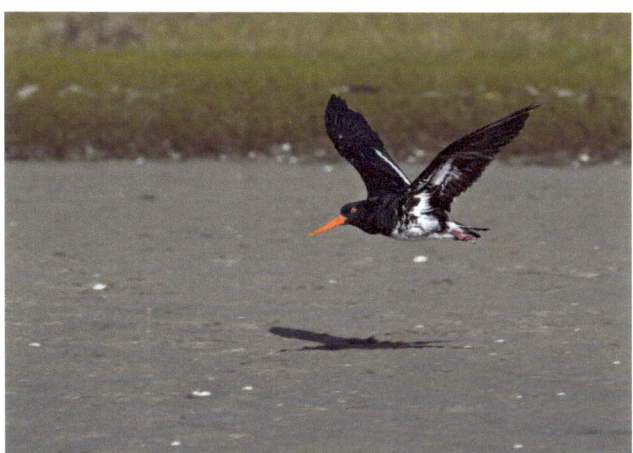

In flight the pied morph VOC shows some of the SIPO's wing pattern, but the underside is is smudgy. Ruakaka, Northland. April.

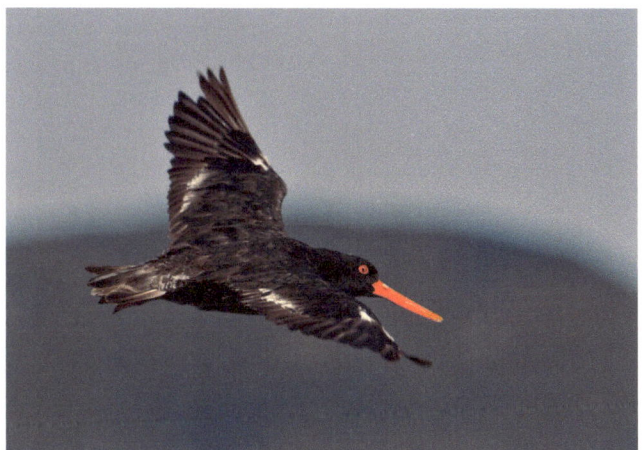

This intermediate morph VOC shows the beginnings of white markings but they are indistinct. Kapowairua, Far North. April

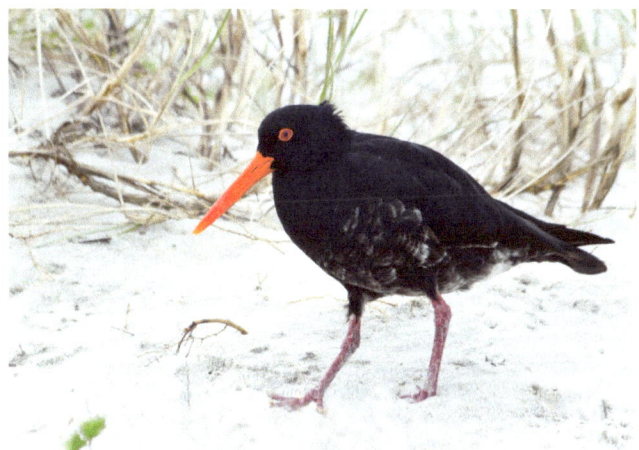

Some intermediate morph birds have no more than flecks of white on the underside. Pakiri, Auckland. November.

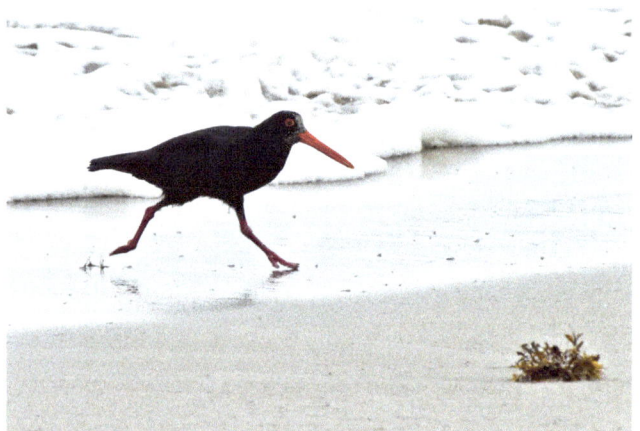

Running to avoid the incoming wave. The sand on its face is from probing for food in the sand. Mount Maunganui. December.

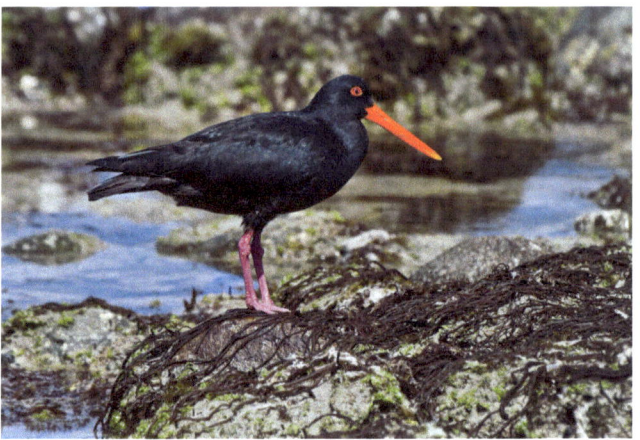

VOC on a rocky shore. Note the yellow bill tip. Maitai Bay, Northland. November.

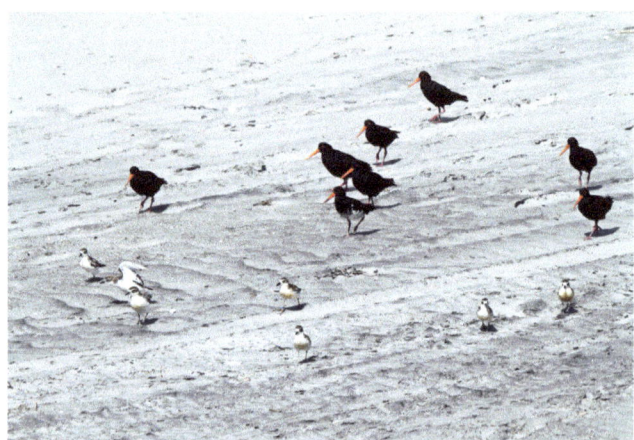

VOCs and NZ dotterels walking together (moving away from a person out of view). Pukehina, Bay of Plenty. January.

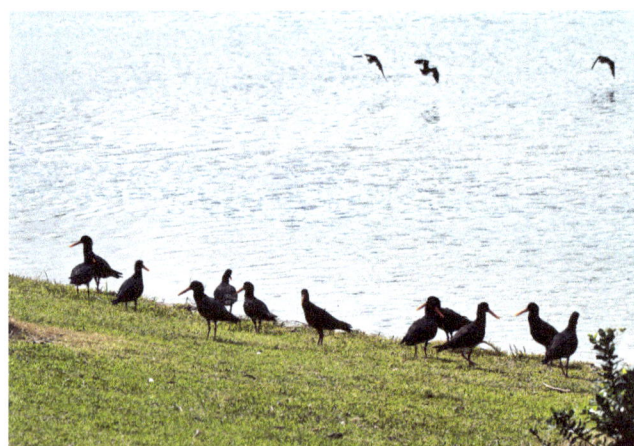

The VOCs in the foreground are alert to my presence but not overly concerned. The SIPOs that were roosting with them have already flown off (top right corner). Ruakaka, Northland. April.

During the September to February breeding season VOCs will be seen in pairs on rocky shorelines or sand spits. On sand spits they often share the same nesting areas as New Zealand dotterels. The two species cohabit reasonably happily but both will fiercely defend the actual nest site from inadvertent intrusion.

After the breeding season finishes VOCs may stay close to the nest area, or may form local flocks of up to about 50 birds. These flocks may be seen near or even with flocks of SIPOs, but a degree of separation will often be apparent.

Their food is very similar to that of the SIPO, but because they have a larger and stronger bill, VOCs can cope with some larger shellfish and are more likely to be seen prising them from rocks. They will also feed along the shoreline on marine worms and bivalves, and can even be seen at times digging for earthworms on beach-front pasture or lawns.

Variable oystercatchers are often more used to the presence of people than SIPOs. They will tolerate being approached fairly closely if this is done slowly and carefully. The birds seem to accept the presence of people as being a normal part of the landscape. When they become uncomfortable they are likely to first walk or even run away before resorting to flight if the threat becomes too great. In the same situation, SIPOs become stressed more quickly and usually just fly away.

Many people have noticed oystercatchers running along the shoreline. They do this when feeding is interrupted by the presence of people, or if threatened by incoming waves.

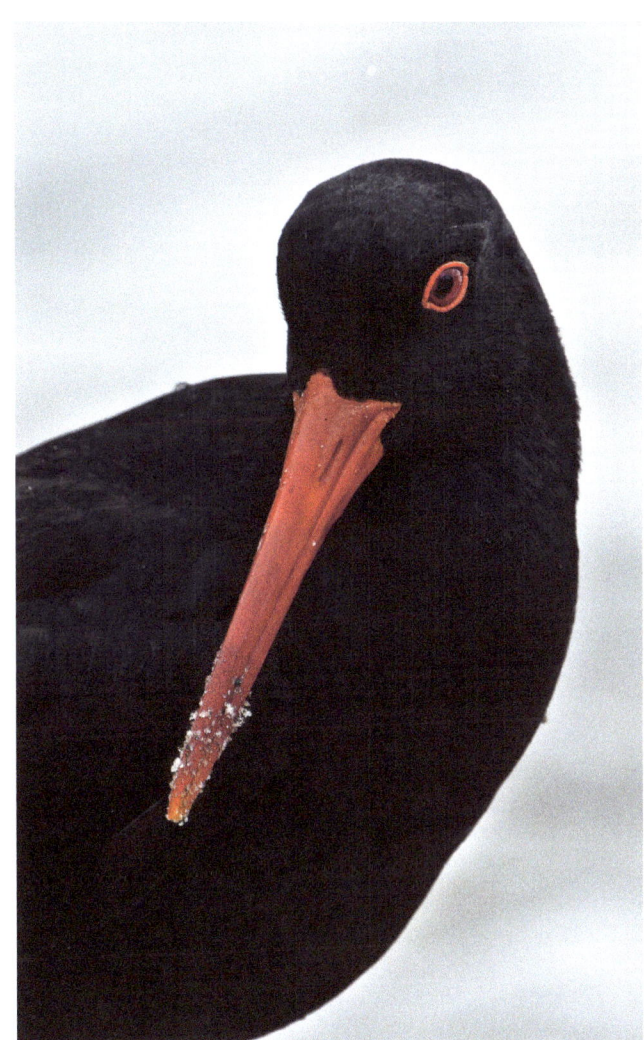

Black morph VOC. Mount Maunganui. December

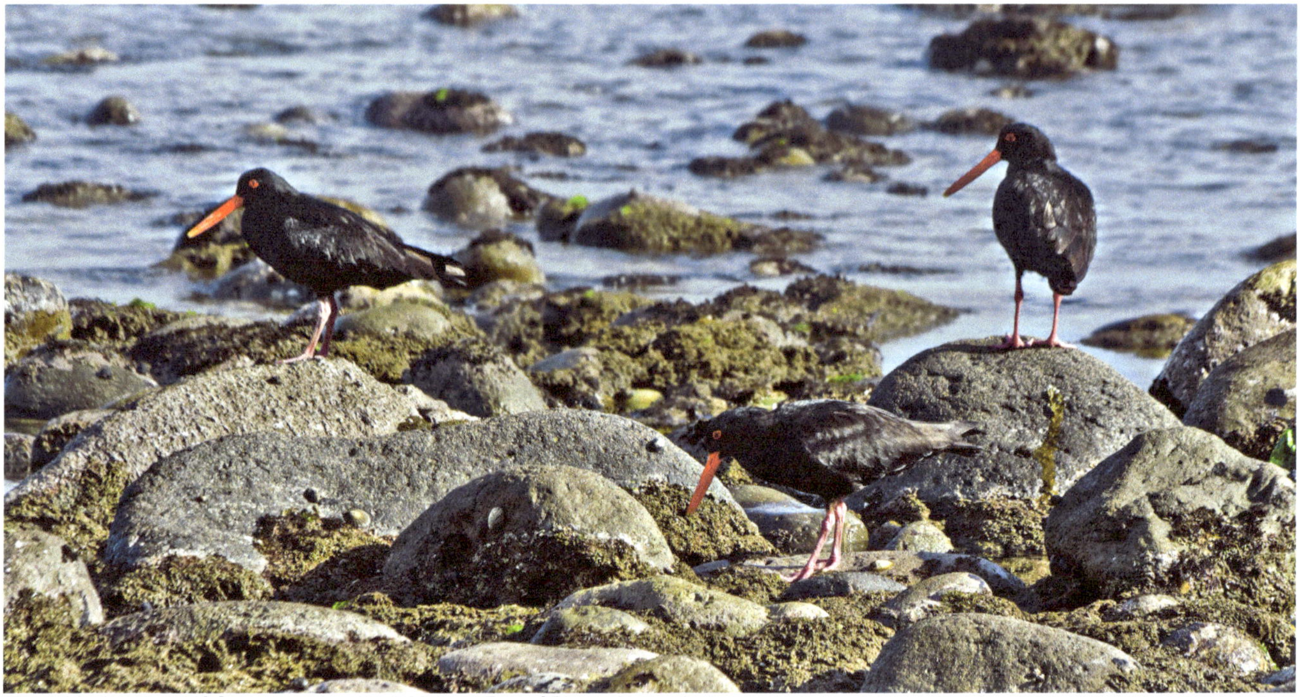

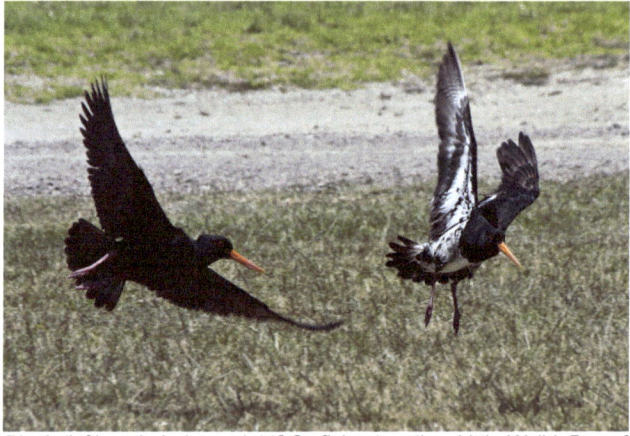

Three black morph VOCs on a rocky shore. Maketu, Bay of Plenty. November.

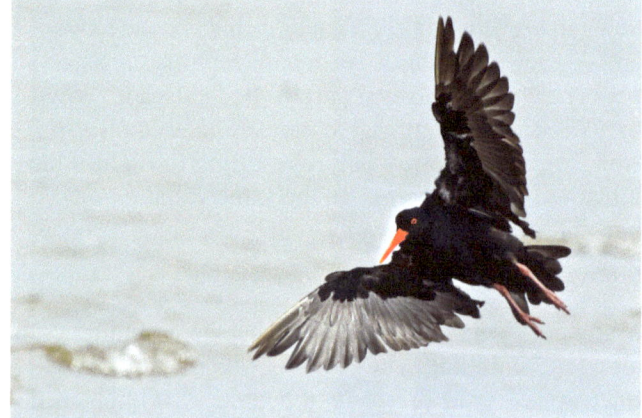

Black (left) and pied morph VOCs flying together. Little Waihi, Bay of Plenty. December.

Black morph VOC coming in to land. Tokerau Beach, Northland. April.

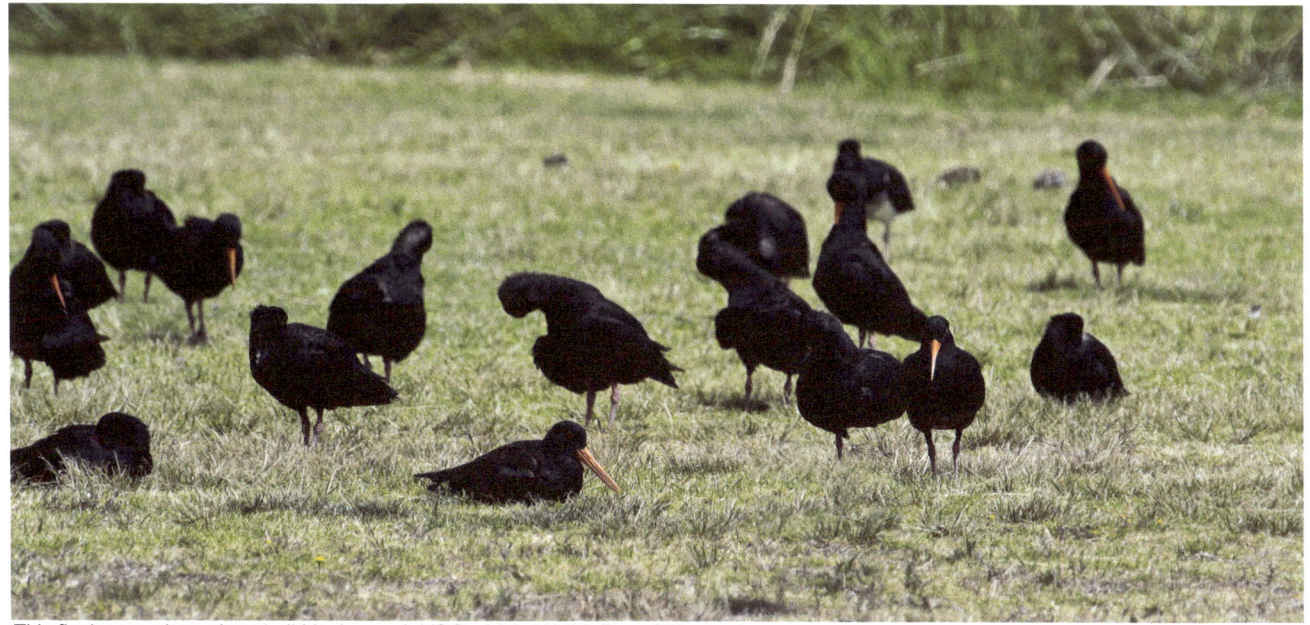

This flock comprises almost all black morph VOCs. Little Waihi, Bay of Plenty. January.

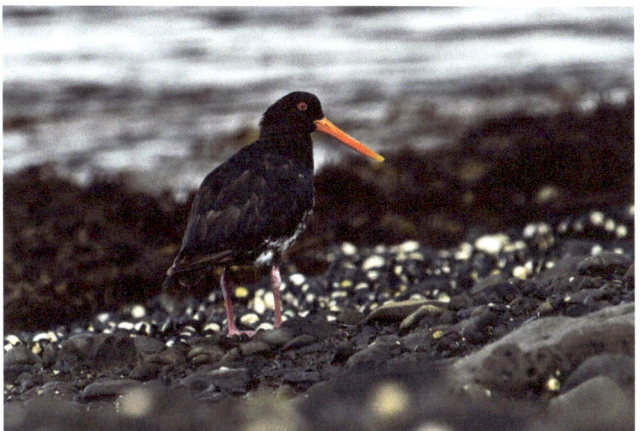

Intermediate morph VOC n a rocky shore habitat, Kapowairua, Far North. April

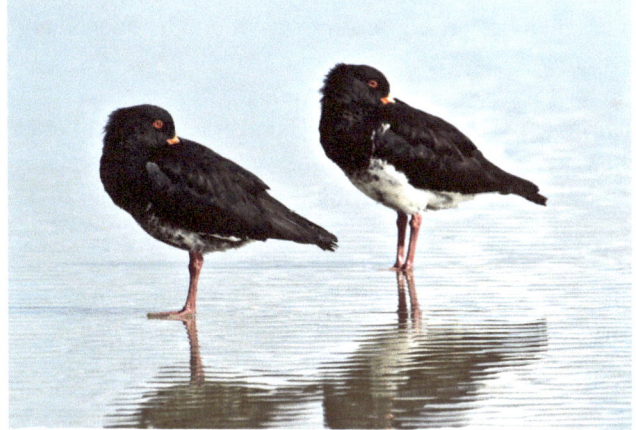

Typical resting pose with the bill tucked under the wing. Intermediate (left) and pied morph VOCs. Ruakaka, Northland. November.

FOOD

New Zealand oystercatchers all have similar diets, with differences governed by variation in habitat and the shape and size of bill. Overall they eat shellfish, crabs, worms, sea anemones and occasionally small fish. In coastal environments the birds rest about two hours either side of high tide and feed, day or night, when the beach or mudflat is exposed at lower tides.

The South Island pied oystercatchers (SIPOs) have a long, straight and very strong bill, with a narrow pointed tip that, when combined with very strong jaw and neck muscles, gives a long reach in the softer substrates of the estuary mudflat or wet pasture habitats. Probing helps to keep the bill worn to a pointed shape, which in turn favours further probing.

When probing in mud or sand the bill will be pushed well into the substrate, slightly open. Shellfish under the sand are caught by the siphon, or if closed, levered against the substrate until they can be lifted out. They may then be carried to firmer ground to be opened and eaten.

Variable oystercatchers (VOCs) also feed by probing but have a slightly shorter, stronger bill that gives them an edge when seeking larger shellfish from rocky or sandy shores.

Small to medium sized bivalves are stabbed where the two halves of the shell meet until the muscle can be forced open by leverage from turning the bill. This feeding method is most successful for birds with a chisel shaped bill tip, worn into shape through repeated action of this kind.

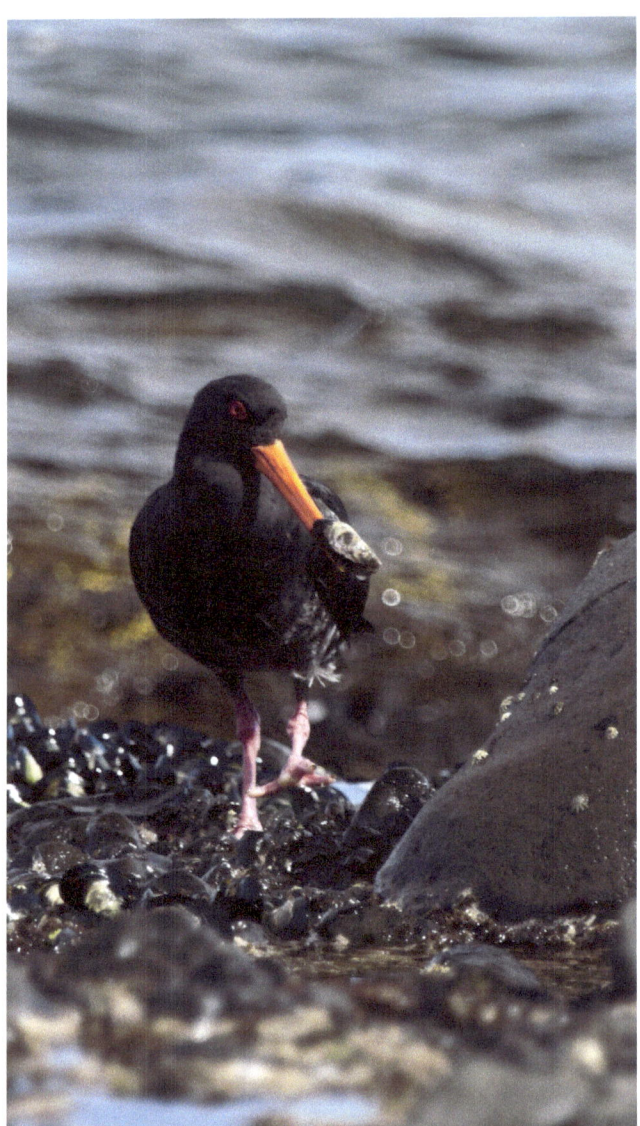

Intermediate morph VOC carrying a mussel from the bed behind. Kapowairua, Far North. April.

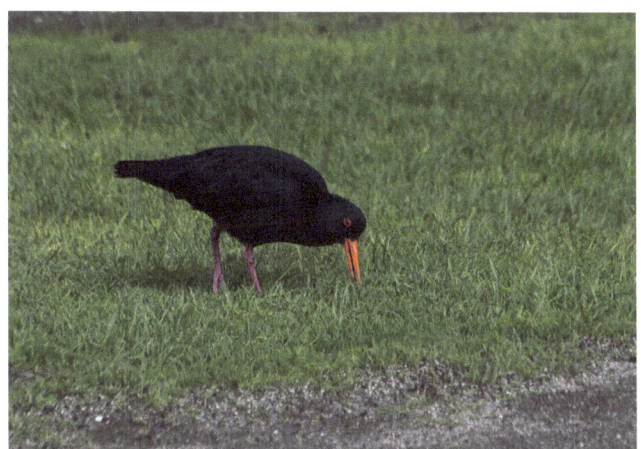
Black morph VOC feeding on worms on a camping ground lawn.
Mount Maunganui. June.

VOCs also attack larger mussels by hammering them on site until they give way. Birds that favour this feeding method have the bill tip worn to a blunt end, which is in turn more effective for further hammering.

They also feed on limpets by loosening them with a sharp vertical blow then pushing or levering the shell with the bill. Chitons are dealt with by a similar sharp blow to the shell-plates or sideways pressure at the edge. Gastropods are opened by starting at the opening and chipping a hole in the opposite shell wall before using that hole to lever against the outside whorl of the shell to break it and eat the meat inside.

In spite of their name, oystercatchers rarely eat oysters. The bill of the SIPO is not really robust enough for the task. VOCs will occasionally tackle an oyster but it takes some time to get to the food and it appears that they prefer mussels if possible.

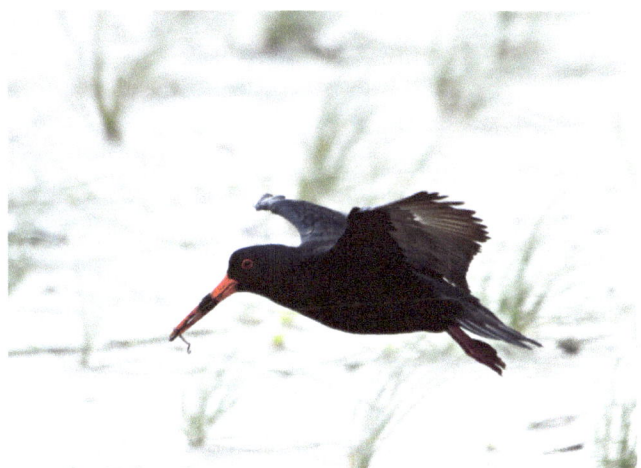
Black morph VOC carrying an earthworm for its chick. Mount Maunganui. January.

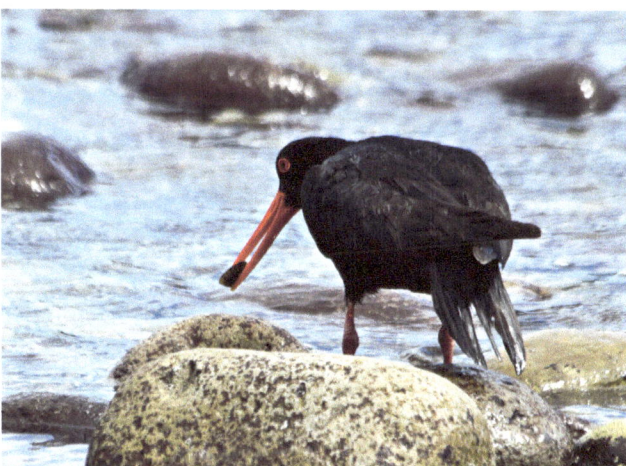
Black morph VOC carrying a limpet. Maketu, Bay of Plenty. November.

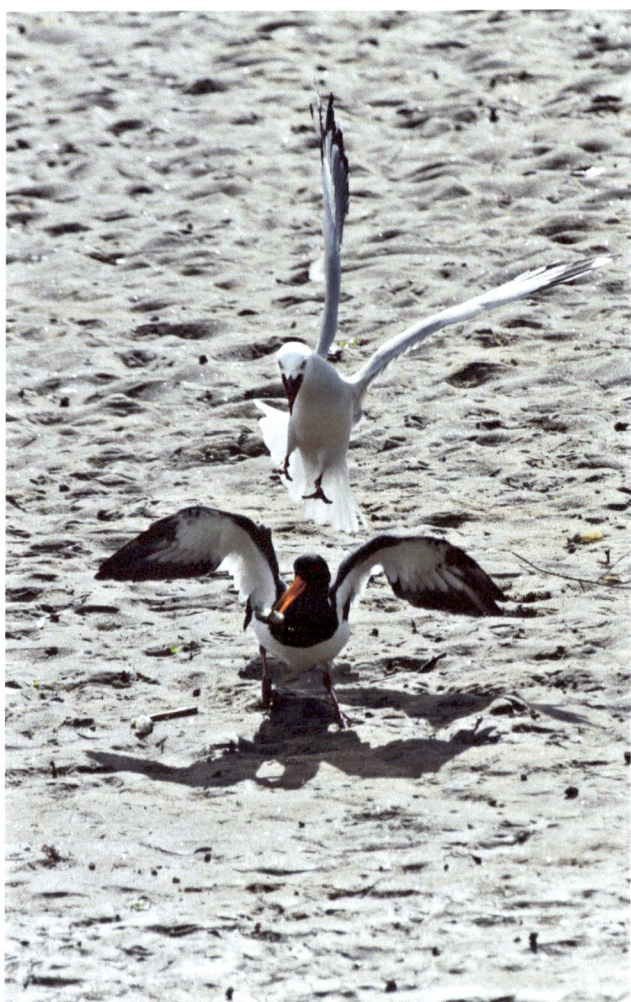

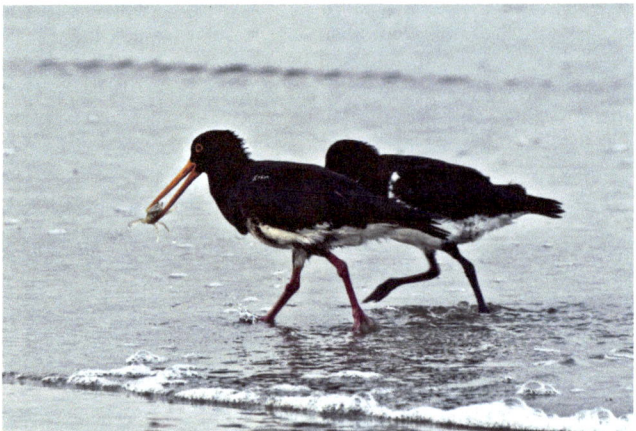

Pied morph VOC carrying a paddle crab. Ruakaka, Northland. April.

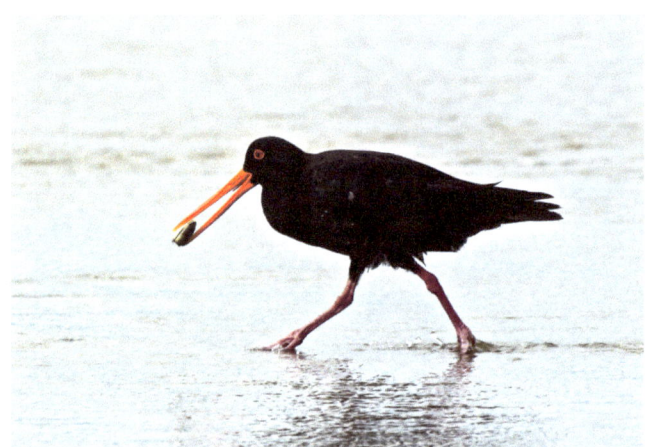

Intermediate morph VOC gripping an unopened tuatua. Tokerau Beach, Northland. April.

Red-billed gulls often try to steal food from oystercatchers. In this case the SIPO dropped the pipi but fought back so that the gull didn't get it either. Maketu, Bay of Plenty. April.

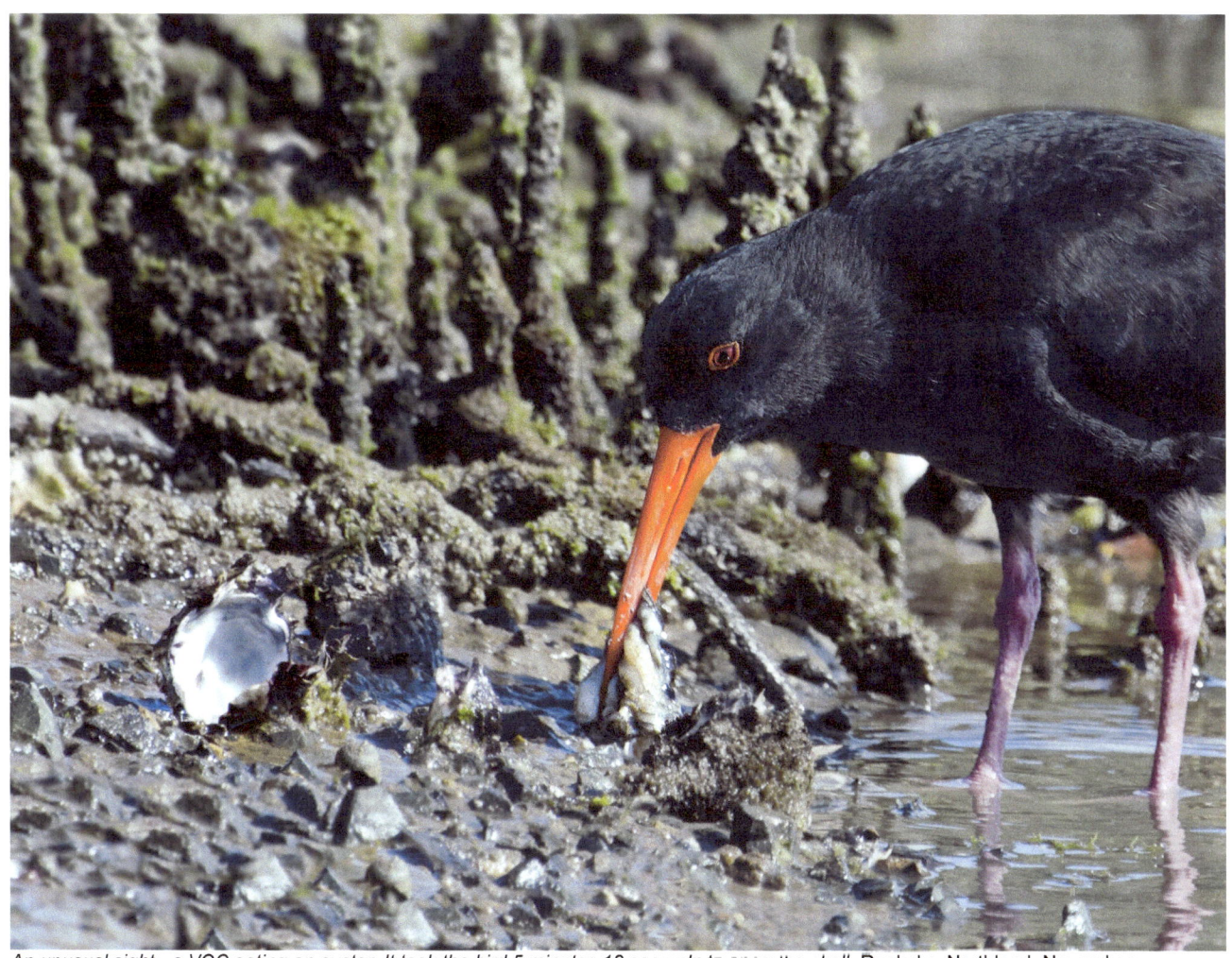

An unusual sight - a VOC eating an oyster It took the bird 5 minutes 18 seconds to open the shell. Ruakaka, Northland. November.

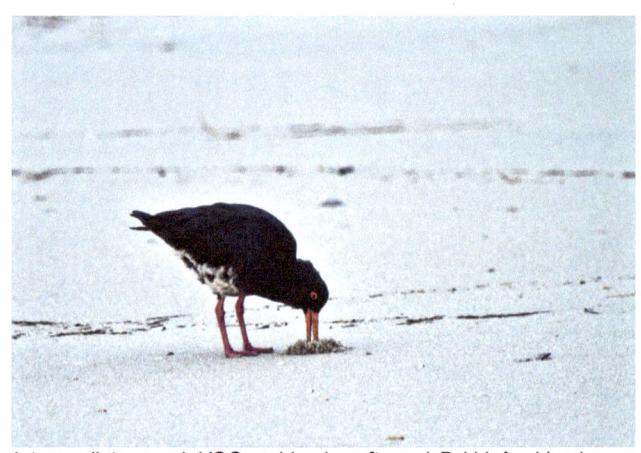

Intermediate morph VOC probing in soft sand. Pakiri, Auckland. April.

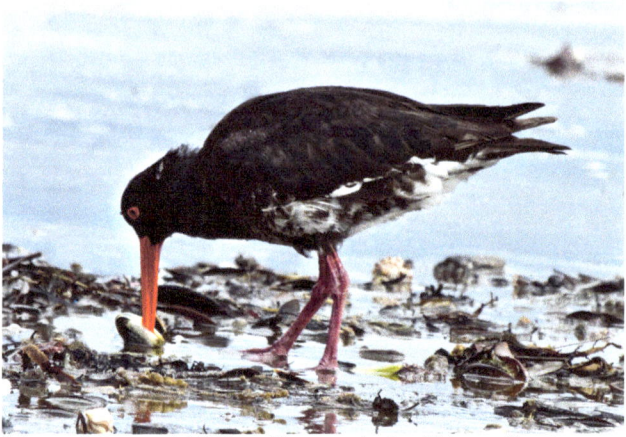

Intermediate morph VOC working on a tuatua. Tokerau Beach, Northland. April.

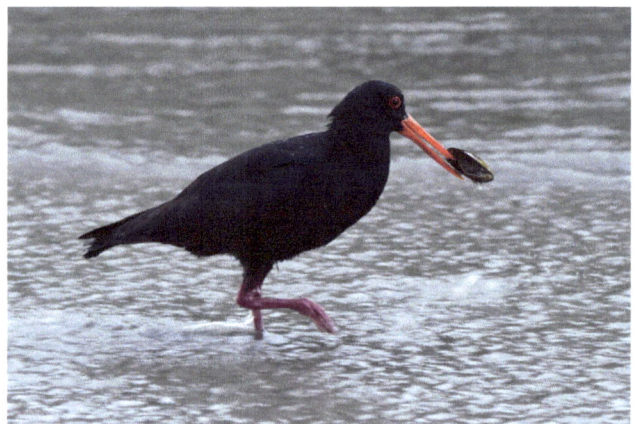

Black morph VOC carrying a mussel that is already open. Mount Maunganui. December.

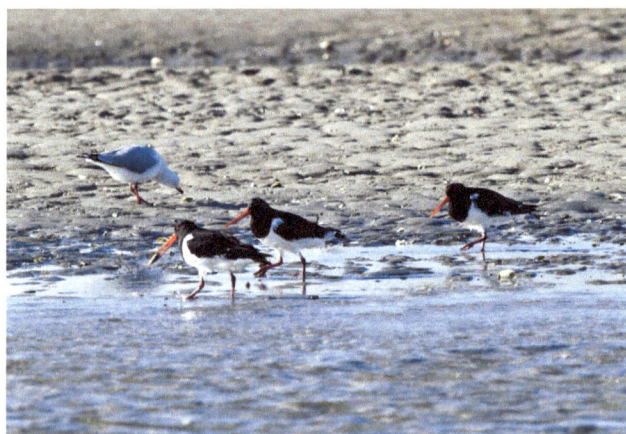

Opportunistic SIPOs hoping to steal the pipi from the successful hunter. Ruakaka, Northland. April.

SOCIAL LIFE

Outside the breeding season South Island pied oystercatchers (SIPOs) are very social birds. They sometimes form flocks of thousands of birds and are rarely seen alone. Variable oystercatchers (VOCs) are less social – they are often found in single pairs, even when not breeding, and when forming flocks these will be small – no more than 150 birds.

Within the flock, oystercatchers maintain a degree of personal space. When the birds are roosting they are still as they rest. If the birds at the edge of the colony move away from a disturbance, they are likely to be attacked by the neighbour whose space they have moved into. This movement can ripple right through the flock.

When feeding the same applies. The flock is loose and birds that stray too close to others will be chased.

When both species are seen together there is often some mixing of the flocks, but on the whole there is a separation between the species. There may be separate flocks, or there may be what appears to be one large flock with a small area where the two species overlap.

As the breeding season approaches, the birds start to pair up and move towards their breeding territories. Those that have bred previously will get together with the last year's partner and move back to the same area they occupied. Both species are monogamous and usually pair for life, although they might over-winter at different places.

Pair bonding and territorial rights are reinforced with rituals known as piping displays which can be used both within the pair itself or aggressively towards other birds encroaching into the territory.

The piping display consists of a distinctive posture where the tail is held low and wide, the wings are held

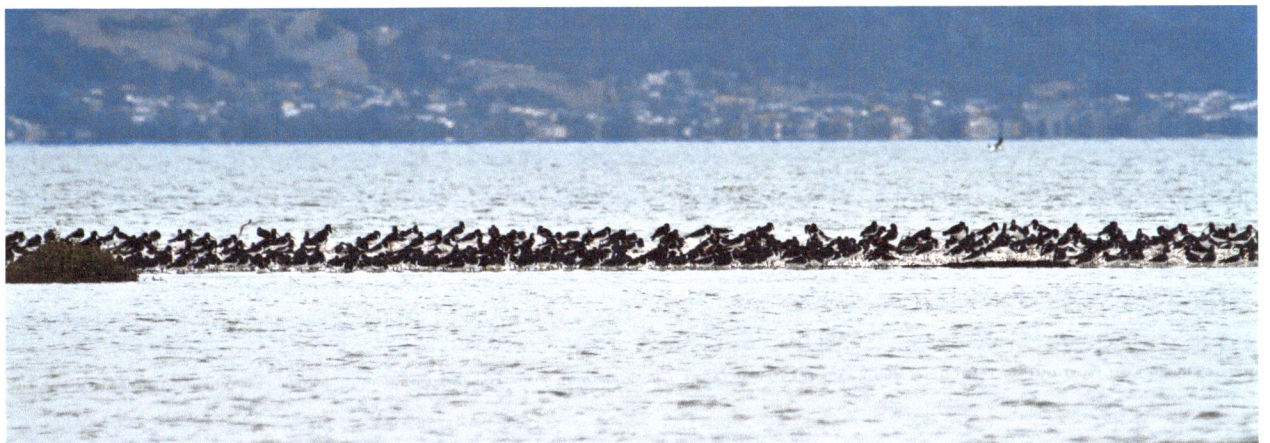

From late summer onwards South Island pied oystercatchers migrate to coastal areas where they congregate in large flocks. The Firth of Thames provides a very large estuary in which the birds feed at low tide, and sandbanks such as the one shown here where the birds roost at high tide. Thousands of birds can be seen here at times. Miranda. March.

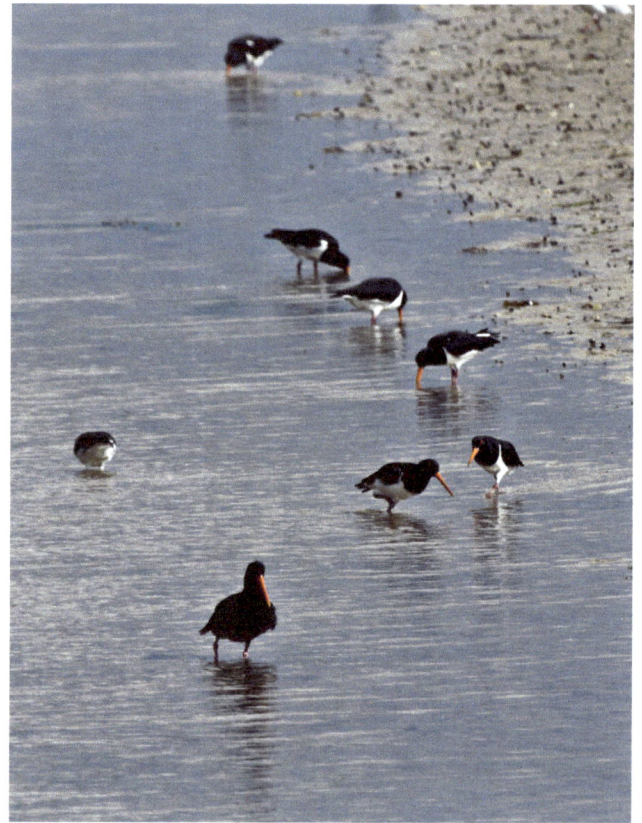

a little out from the body, the neck is arched and the bill is vertical. The bird runs along in this position making a distinct "piping" call as it goes. Birds piping together move in unison, including sudden changes of direction of 90 to 180 degrees.

When the piping display is courtship related the recipient of the display is likely to turn towards the initiator and/or they will run together. The display may encourage others to join in so that several pairs are displaying together. If the pair flies off, they will fly close together.

When the display is aggressive, the pair will be clearly chasing another bird or birds. This display may end in actual fighting.

Another gesture that is often seen is a head-bob. It is a sharp upwards movement of the head that may be repeated but is unclear what its message is. It is clearly not always related to alarm or courtship. It may simply be about getting a better view of the surroundings and can even be seen in juveniles.

Black morph VOC and a group of SIPO at low tide. Maketu, Bay of Plenty. April.

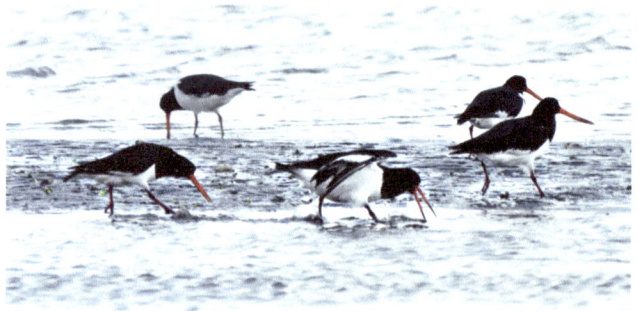

SIPO chasing another SIPO. Little Waihi, Bay of Plenty. August.

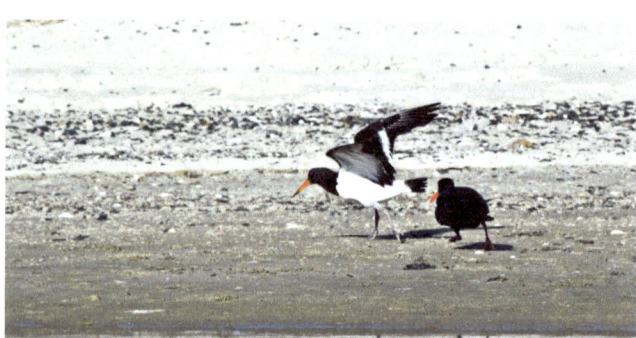

Black morph VOC chasing a SIPO. Ruakaka, Northland. April.

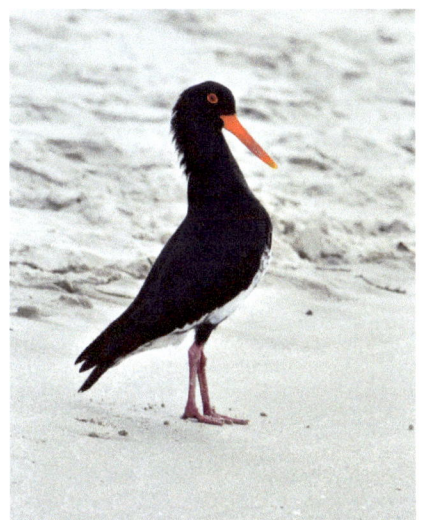

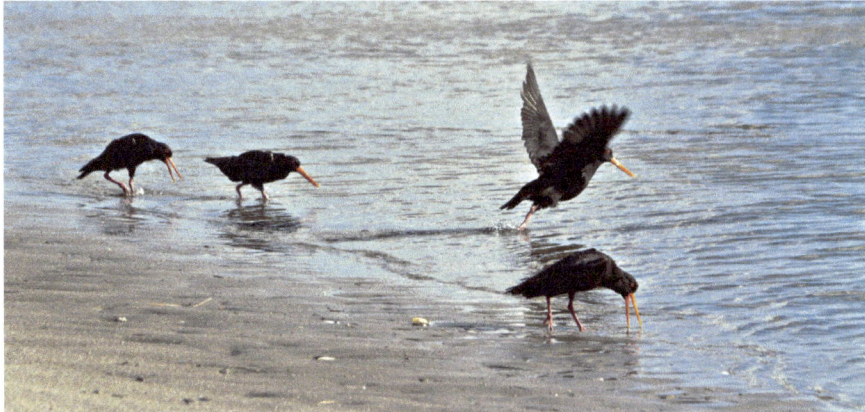

Pukehina, Bay of Plenty. January.

Above. Head bob - a sharp, momentary, upwards movement of the head. Intermediate morph VOC. Ruakaka, Northland. November.

Below. Pair of intermediate morph VOCs flying together. Pukehina, Bay of Plenty. December.

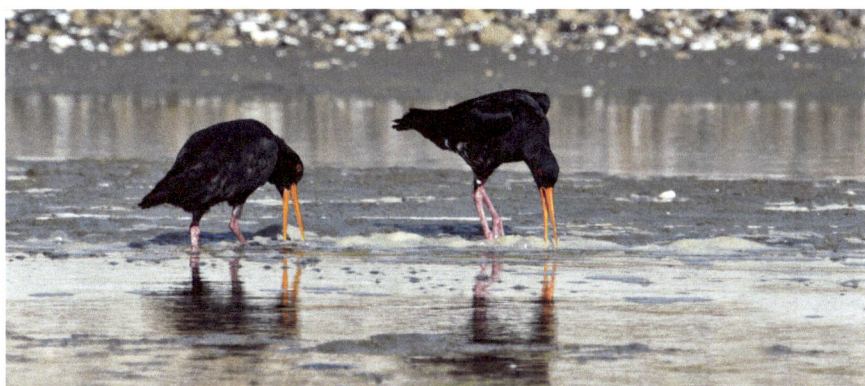

Above and below Ruakaka, Northland. April.

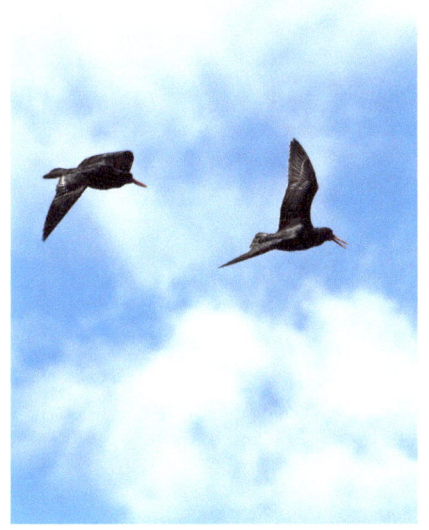

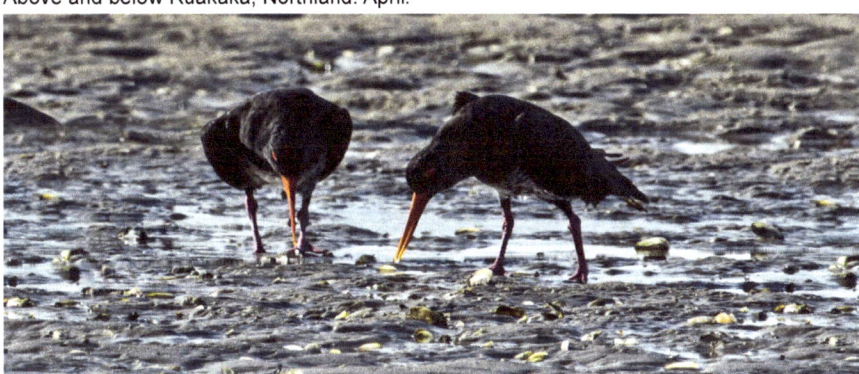

Three views of VOC piping displays (above).

NESTING

Both species of oystercatcher nest in a simple hollow or scrape in the ground or sand. It may be lined with a few pebbles or twigs, or may be completely bare. It is likely to be close to a branch or some other "marker" that provides a bit of shelter and helps returning birds locate it. Oystercatchers are highly territorial and nests may be 200m to more than 1km apart.

The male bird is a little smaller than the female, with a shorter bill that is a little brighter or more red in colour. The difference is minimal and is not always easy to detect when observing the birds. Once paired, birds usually nest in the same territory each year and will stay together for life.

The South Island pied oystercatcher nests inland in river beds, adjacent land, ploughed areas or cultivated pasture. There are usually 2 eggs about 56mm long, laid from August through to November or December. Both parents share the incubation for 24-27 days.

The variable oystercatcher usually nests in the sand just above high tide mark. Nests are often on sand-spits or sometimes found on rocks. There are usually 2-3 eggs about 58mm long, laid from October through to January or February. The eggs are incubated by both parents for 27-28 days.

The nest and its adjacent territory is fiercely defended by both parents. While one bird sits on the nest, the other keeps watch for predators. Any intruders will be attacked and chased away by both parents. The pair may also lure intruders away with strategies such as broken wing displays or pretending to sit on a "dummy" nest.

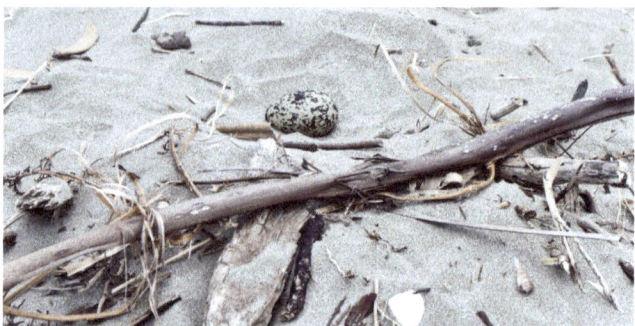

Typical VOC nest - a simple hollow near some beach debris. The single egg was probably not yet being incubated so the parent had taken a break, but was near by. Ohope, Bay of Plenty. December.

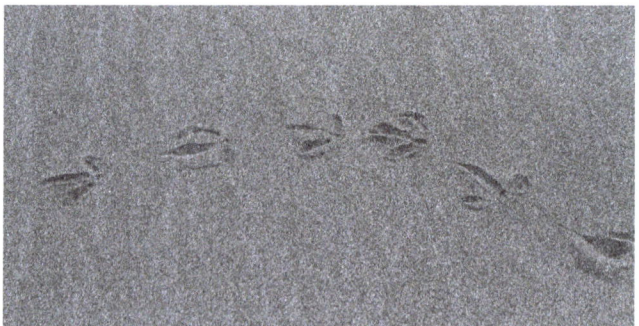

Following the footprints backwards meant I could find the nest to view it while it was unattended. I only had a moment before I was seen by the absent parent and needed to leave.

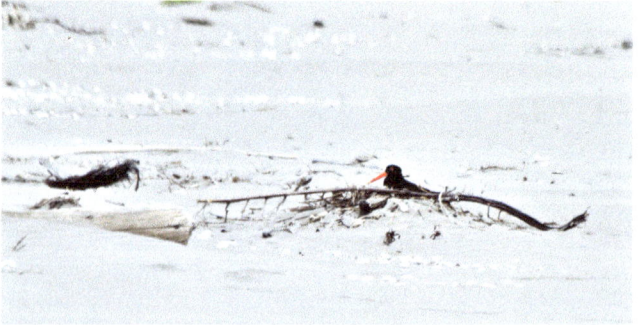

Parent back on the nest above after I moved away.

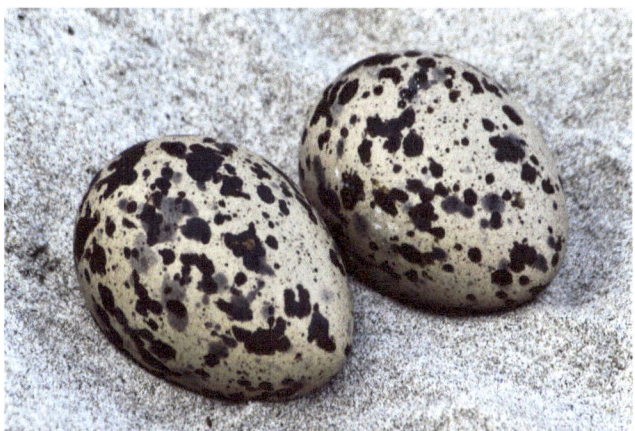

Close up of eggs from a different nest. A group of people walking and talking failed to notice the VOC's alarm calls and someone nearly walked on the nest. Luckily it was seen in time. Otago Peninsular. December.

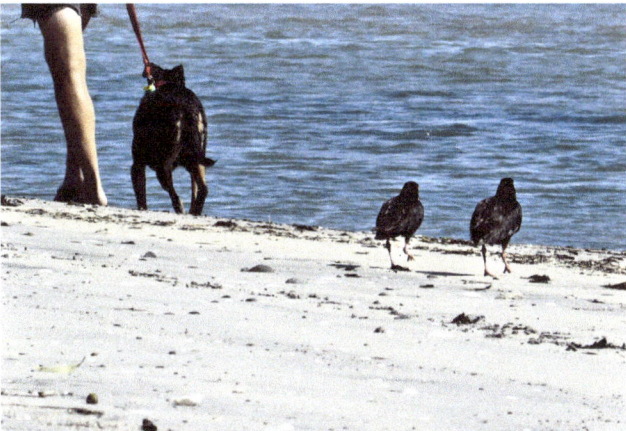

This dog being walked on a lead near the waterline so was no threat to the two birds to the right of the photo. They didn't know that though and were "seeing it off" as much as they could. Loose dogs are one of the main threats to the conservation of endangered ground nesting birds such as the VOC and also the New Zealand dotterel that shares this habitat.

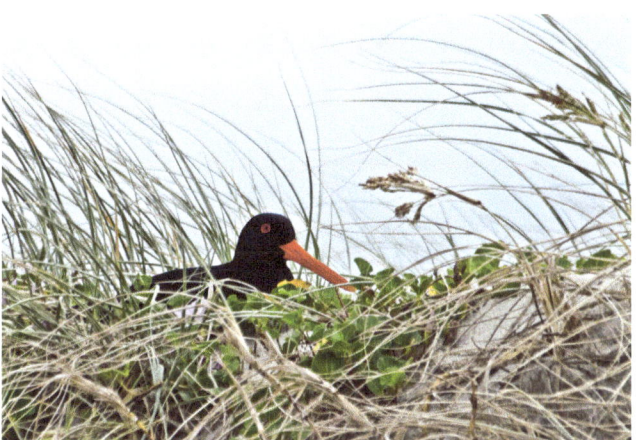

This VOC has a good location for its nest - up on a sand dune where it has a good view of the surrounding area and is safe from being walked on or run over. Pakiri, Auckland. November.

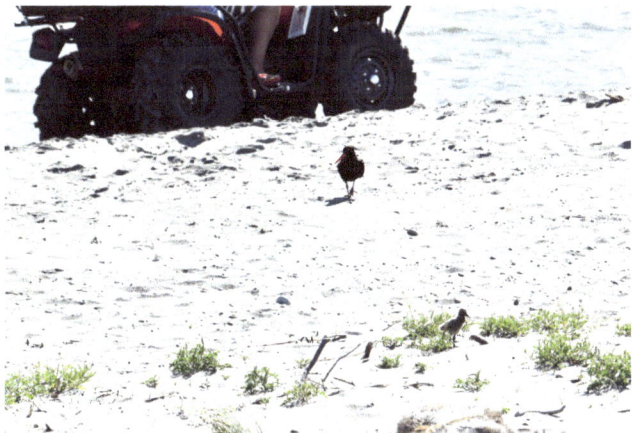

Quad bikes and other vehicles are also an extreme threat to nests and young such as the VOC chick in the right foreground. This rider stayed out of the fenced nesting area, but of course the birds don't understand the purpose of the fences and are still vulnerable to having nests and chicks run over.

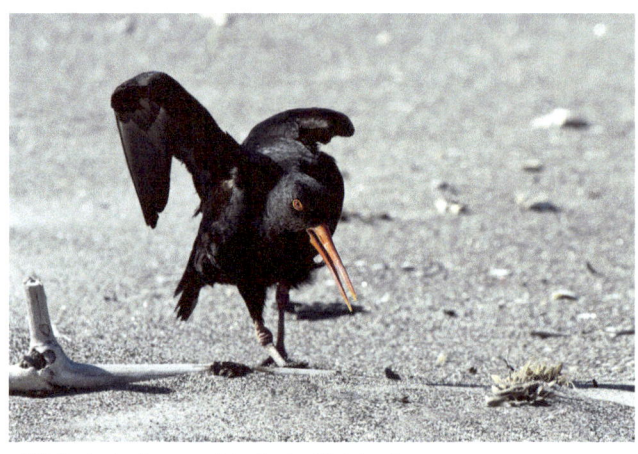
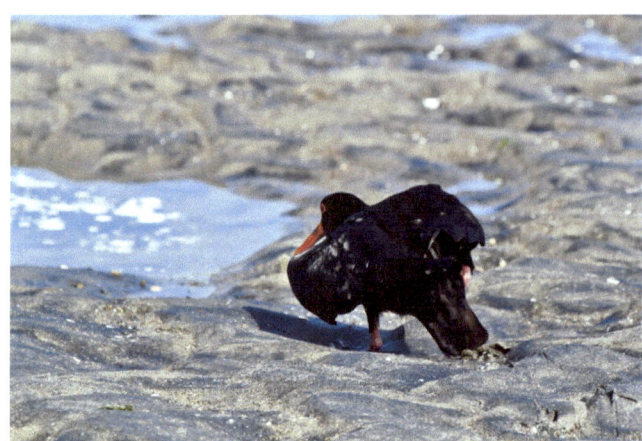

VOC strategies used to deal with intruders:
> *Above left: Trying to chase the intruder away.*
> *Above right: A broken wing display to lead the intruder away.*
> *Below left: A 'dummy nest' to take the intruder's attention away from the real nest. The bird nestled alongside its mate into the wet sand and glowered at me while hoping I would go away, which I did.*
> *Below right: Outright aggression. The reef heron happened to land where the VOC family was feeding and the adult VOCs succeeded in chasing it away.*

All Pukehina, Bay of Plenty. Below right January. Others December.

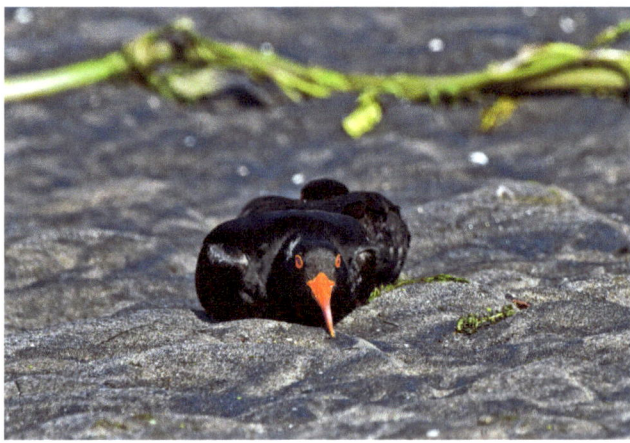
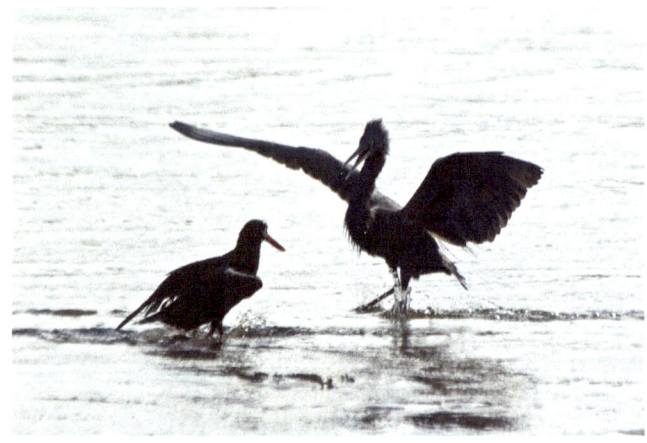

RAISING THE FAMILY

The chicks are well developed at the time of hatching and leave the nest within a day or two. Both parents actively care for and feed them until they fledge at about six weeks old.

As the juveniles mature they become more independent, but still stay with the family group and receive help with feeding for several more weeks or even months. The skills needed to open shells are taught to them by the parents and take some time to master before the young become fully independent.

When feeding, the family may stay close together, or may separate out. Often one parent stays with the chicks while the other forages for food further away. When the chicks are very small they are fed directly by the parents who bring the food to them. As they grow they start to follow their parents to the water's edge and begin poking around for themselves in between being fed.

When the parent brings food, at first it just feeds the chick directly from bill to bill. Later it will bring a whole shell and open it with the chick watching in its first lessons on how to obtain food. The parent will open the shell, possibly eat some itself, then leave the rest for the chick to eat while the parent goes off looking for more.

When there are two or three chicks in the family, the dominant one will try to push the others away. The parents seem happy enough to simply feed whoever is closest at the time.

While in the care of the parents the young are actively protected as well as fed. When danger threatens the chick will run then hide near some driftwood, vegetation or similar, using its camouflaged colouring as best it can, while the parents chase the intruder or try to lure it away.

If one parent is away feeding, the first alarm call of the adult with the young will bring it back immediately to help with protection of the family.

Some family groups stay together over the first winter with the young continuing to beg for food. Other groups may disperse by the end of the breeding season. Sometimes the parents will enforce the independence of the young by chasing them away.

The birds mature and begin breeding in their fourth year. Until then, they will tend to stay in flocks in seashore or estuary habitats.

The comments and photos on this and the following pages relate to my observation of variable oystercatchers. It is most likely that South Island pied oystercatchers follow similar behaviours although their inland habitat may create some differences – eg the food is not only marine based as it is with VOCs.

Getting close enough to observe and photograph VOCs is reasonably easy in well-populated locations. They are used to people in the environment and so long as I keep still they quickly forget about me. By moving up one step at a time, or wriggling on my knees, I am sometimes able to get surprisingly close to the birds.

The following pages illustrate some of the family groups I have watched.

The photos on these two pages are from Otarawairere, near Whakatane in the Bay of Plenty. Despite the steep access track, it's a well-loved spot for the locals and the VOCs here were clearly well-used to people.

The chicks were initially more nervous of me than the parents were, but when the parents sat down to rest they also relaxed and continued poking around in the rocks or resting with the adults. The photos were taken in February. It is likely that these chicks are a second clutch following the loss of the early season clutch.

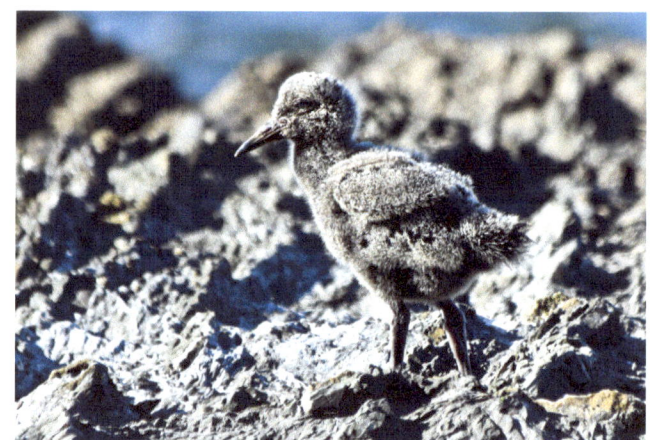

A handsome little fellow.

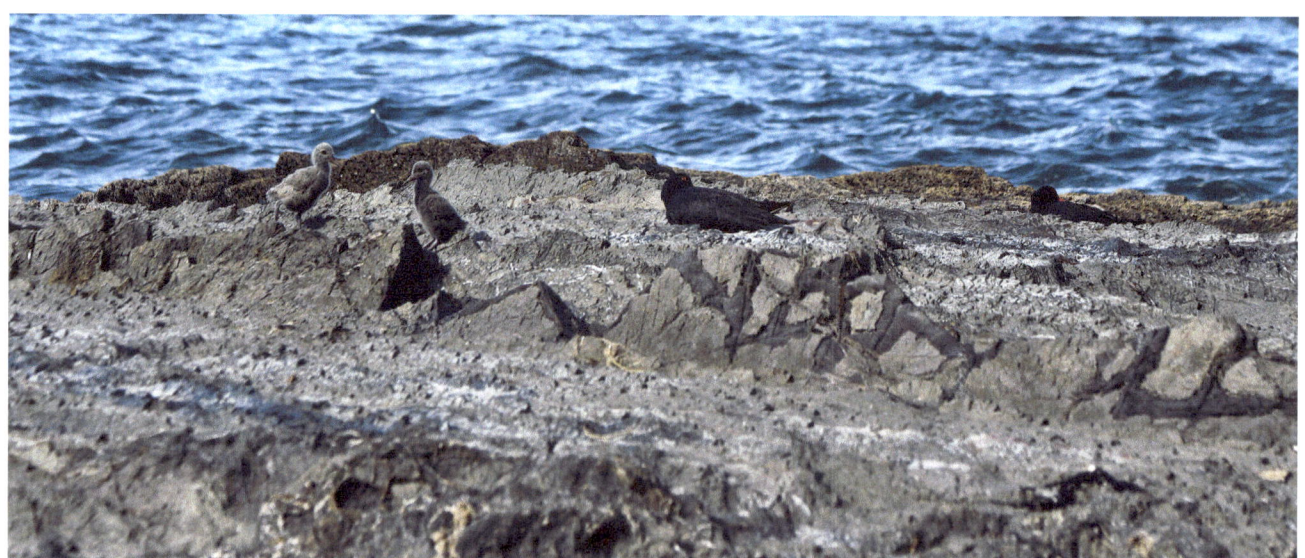

Rocky shore habitat - the two chicks are very well camouflaged and the parents can also be surprisingly hard to see.

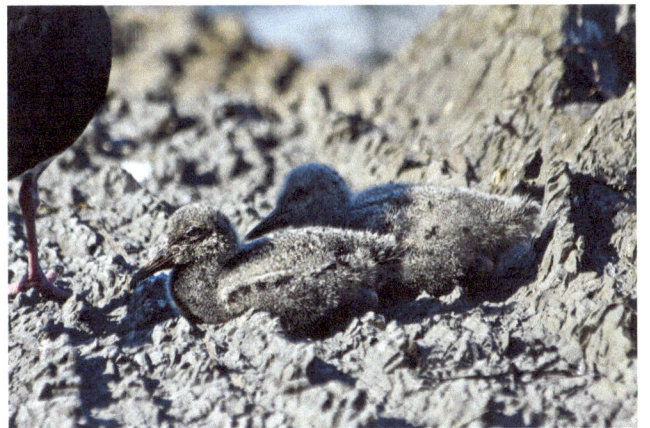
Taking a nap.

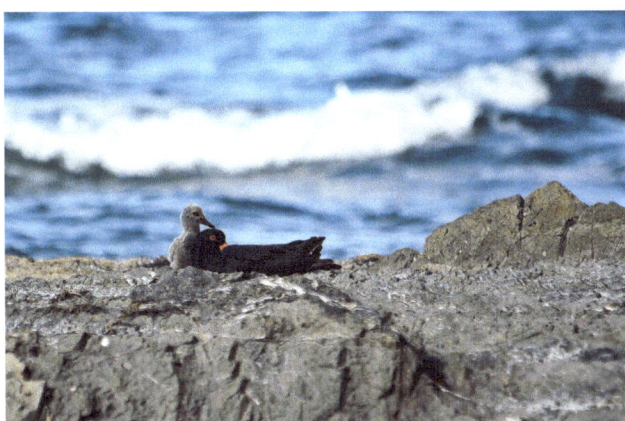
Seeking security by cuddling up to an adult.

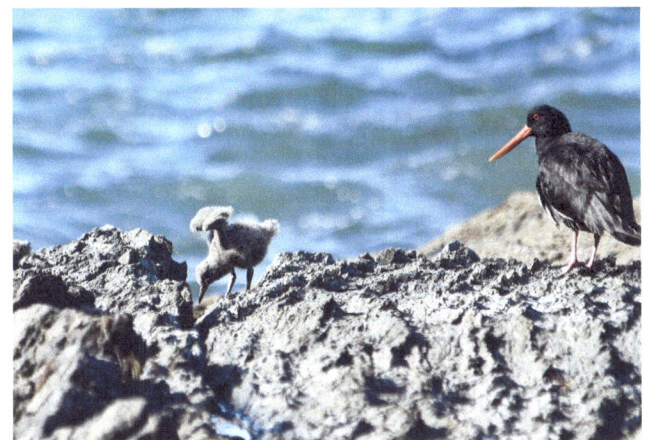
Even little wings can be useful when crossing a chasm in the rocks.

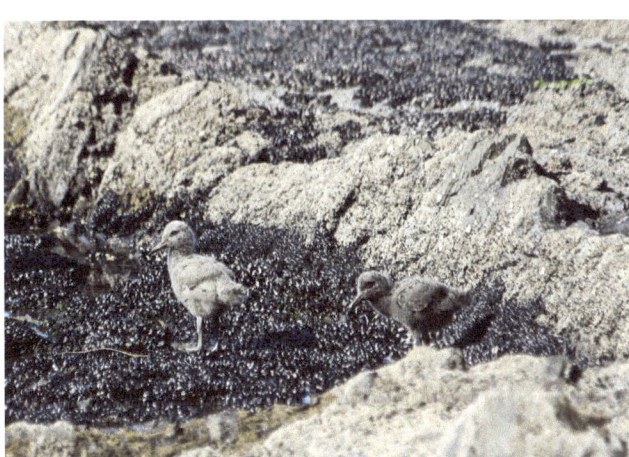
Walking across a bed of small mussels – a larger species will be a favourite food in the future.

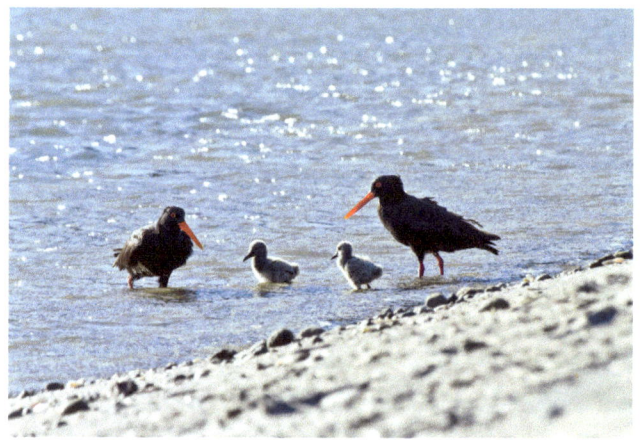

A family group in the estuary shallows at low tide.

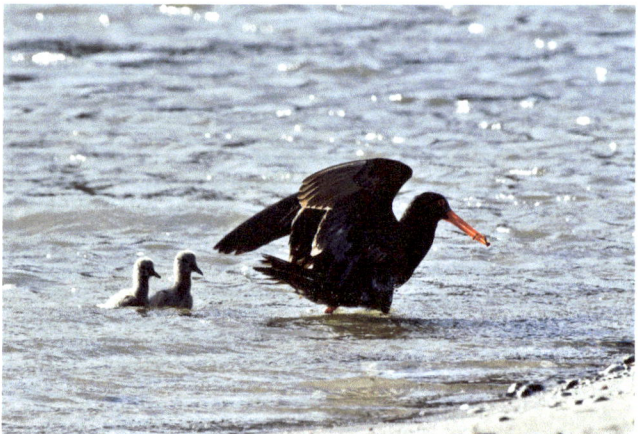

Food is taken to the shoreline for the chicks while they follow.

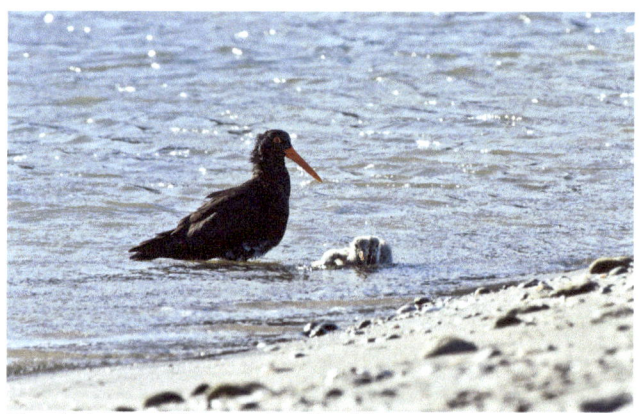

The chicks squabble over who will get the worm.

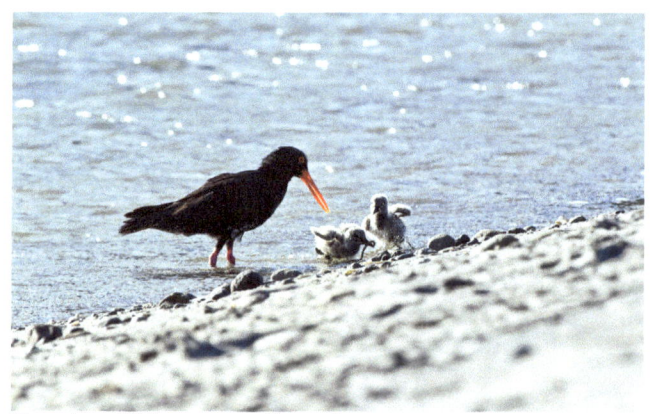

The winner! This sequence December.

28

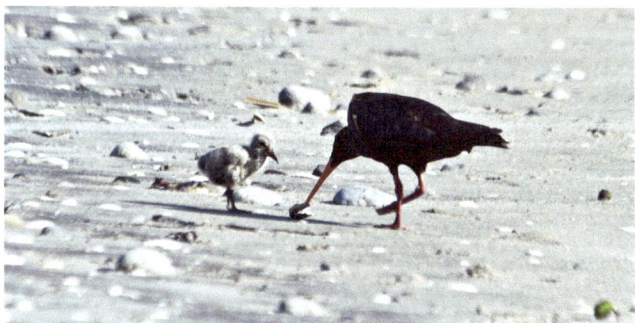
The chick watches while the shell is opened for it.

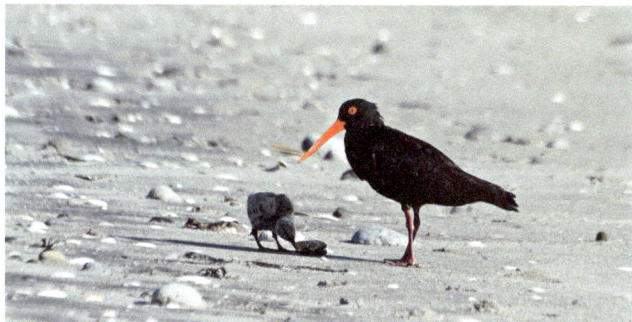
The parent watches while the chick takes over and starts feeding.

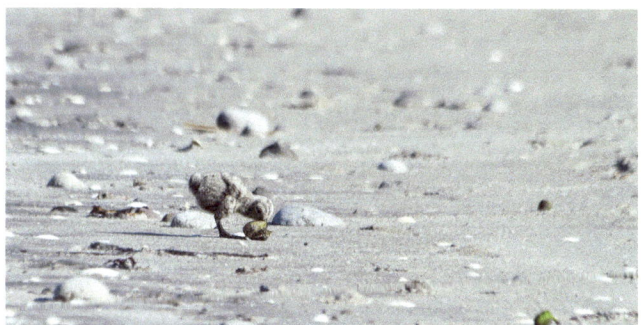
The chick is left to continue working at the shell while the parent looks for more food. This sequence January.

Pukehina in the Bay of Plenty has a sand spit that is home to a colony of VOCs as well as endangered New Zealand dotterels. The adjacent estuary provides a good feeding ground and there is enough space for each of the species to cohabit with the other.

The area is also a popular ocean beach and fishing spot so there are a lot of people around. This means the birds are reasonably used to the presence of people, although the dotterels are far less tolerant than the oystercatchers.

When watching the oystercatchers, it's important to be aware of the dotterels as well. If they spend too long calling their alarm the unattended eggs or chicks may suffer so awareness of this is important.

The colony of VOCs at this location usually has several families with young at different ages. They are illustrated on these two pages and overleaf.

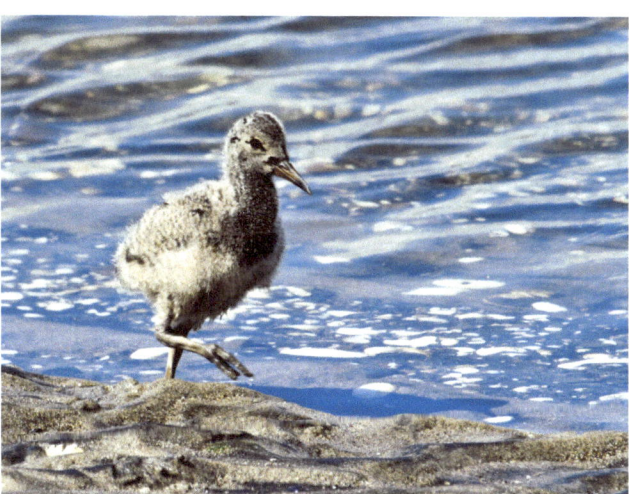
Striding out along the water-line. December.

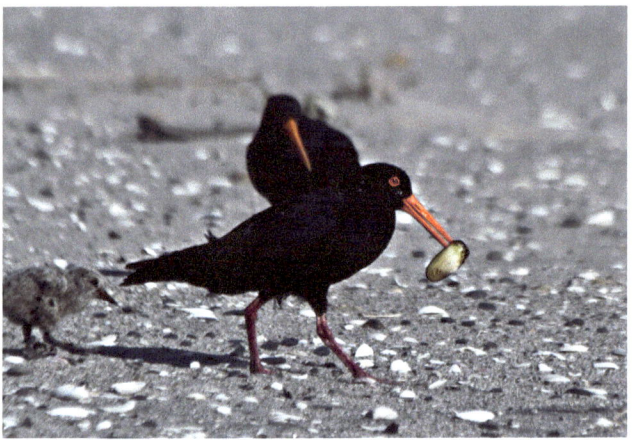

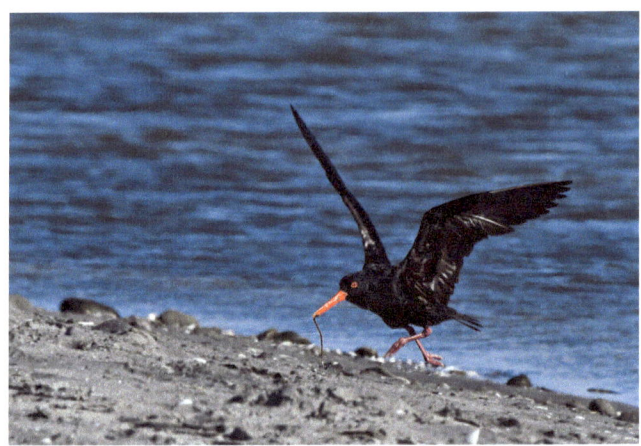

Bringing food - a worm (above right) and a pipi (above). The pipi is held by its own muscle. Both December.

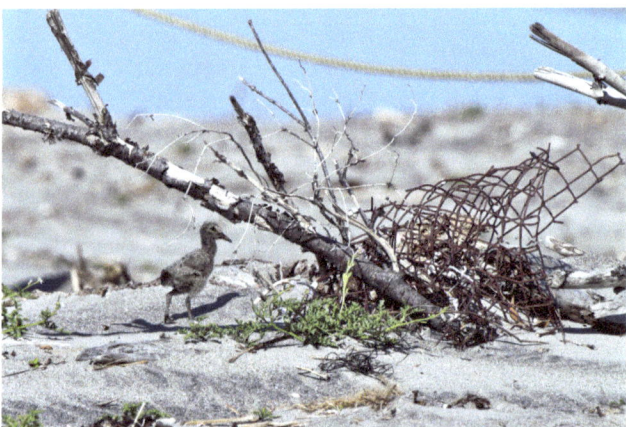

Left alone while its parents were foraging, this chick was nervous and hiding near some rubbish. When an unrelated oystercatcher walking by was unconcerned about me, the chick relaxed and started foraging until its parents returned. December.

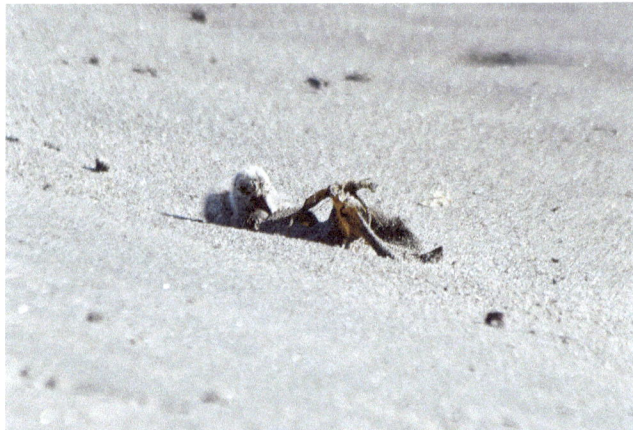

When the family group was disturbed by several other oyster-catchers flying in, this chick ran to hide next to a piece of kelp while its parents chased the intruders away using an aggressive piping display. January.

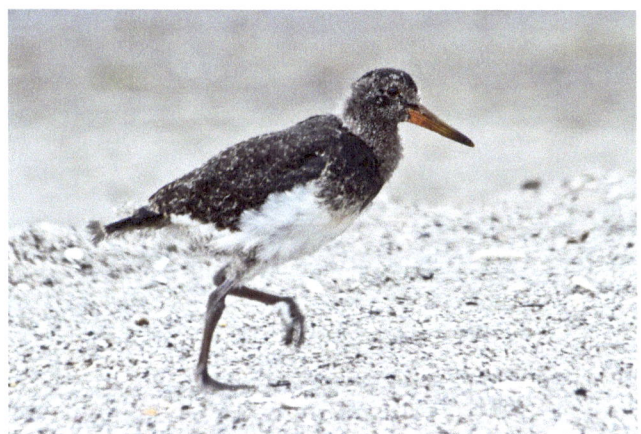

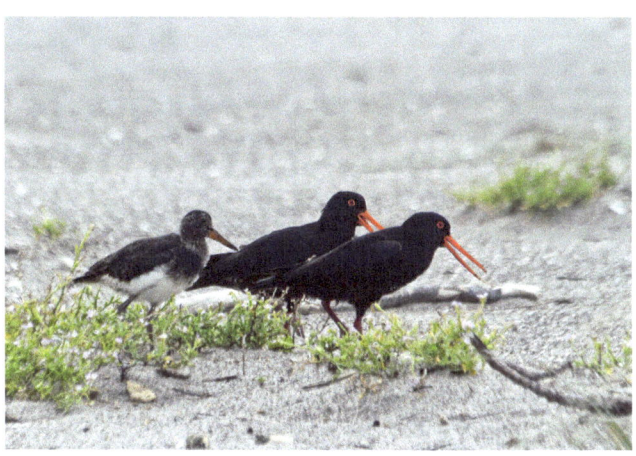

Partly fledged pied morph juvenile (above), and with its intermediate morph parents (above right). January.

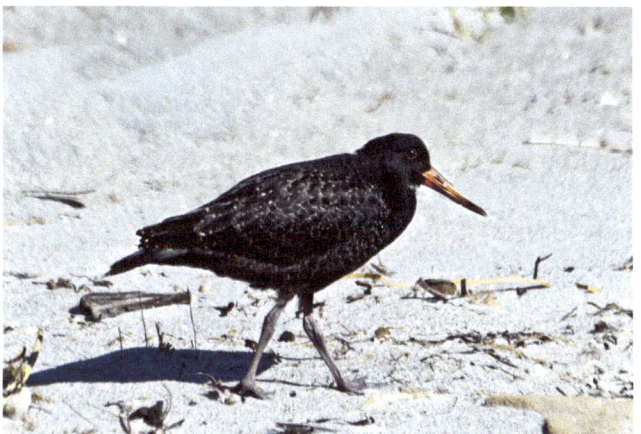

Fully fledged immature black morph. The colours of the bill, legs and feathers are not as bright as those of an adult bird and will continue to mature over the next three years along with its eye colour (from brown to yellow to orange-red) and its legs and bill. January.

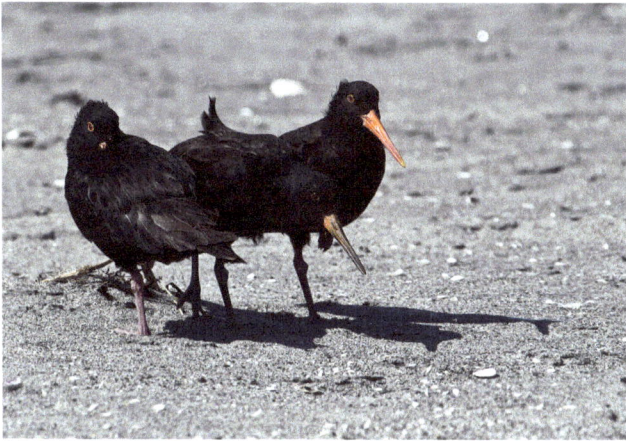

The immature bird (centre) stays with its parents and continues to beg for food from them, but is by now able to feed itself as well. It will be independent by the following spring, having had a long period to learn the skills taught to it by its parents. All black morph. January.

The main beach at Mount Maunganui has a resident pair of VOCs that go about their daily lives largely unobserved by the thousands of people who use the beach. The birds nest in the area that encompasses the beach in front of the camping ground and the rocks at the beginning of the base of "The Mount".

These rocks are covered in mussels and so provide a ready source of food. The lawns at the camping ground also provide a good supply of worms.

The presence of so many people means that the birds are relaxed about being watched. On one occasion I was quietly moving forward one step at a time. The parent was resting about 7 metres to my left and the chick about 7 metres to my right. One step too far made the parent wake up, walk over to the chick to sit next to it, and go back to sleep. They remained relaxed while I went even closer.

This environment has both sandy beach and rocky shore. The downside is that the urban nature of area brings predators. Most years seem to see only one chick raised successfully.

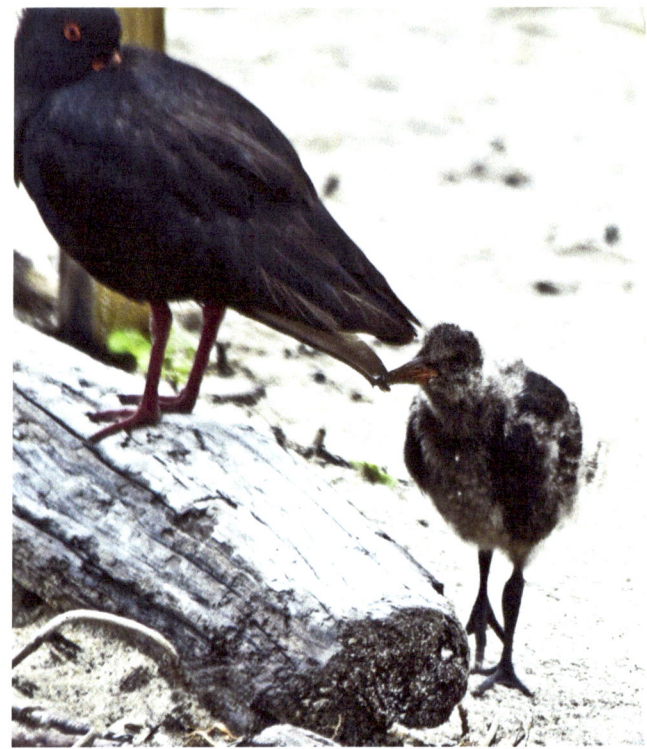

Nibbling the tail feathers of a resting parent. January.

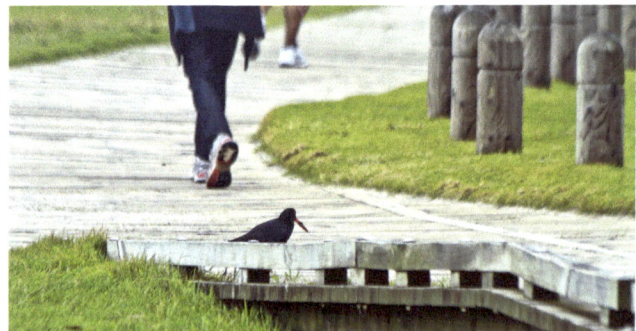

Walking from the beach, across the busy boardwalk, to the camping ground lawn to look for worms. January.

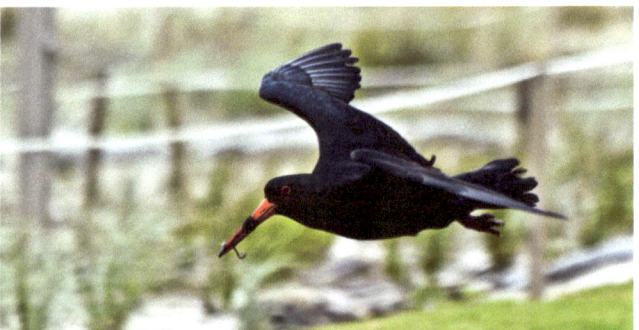

15 minutes later the bird was back with a worm for the chick. The black on the bird's bill shows how far it probed to get the worms.

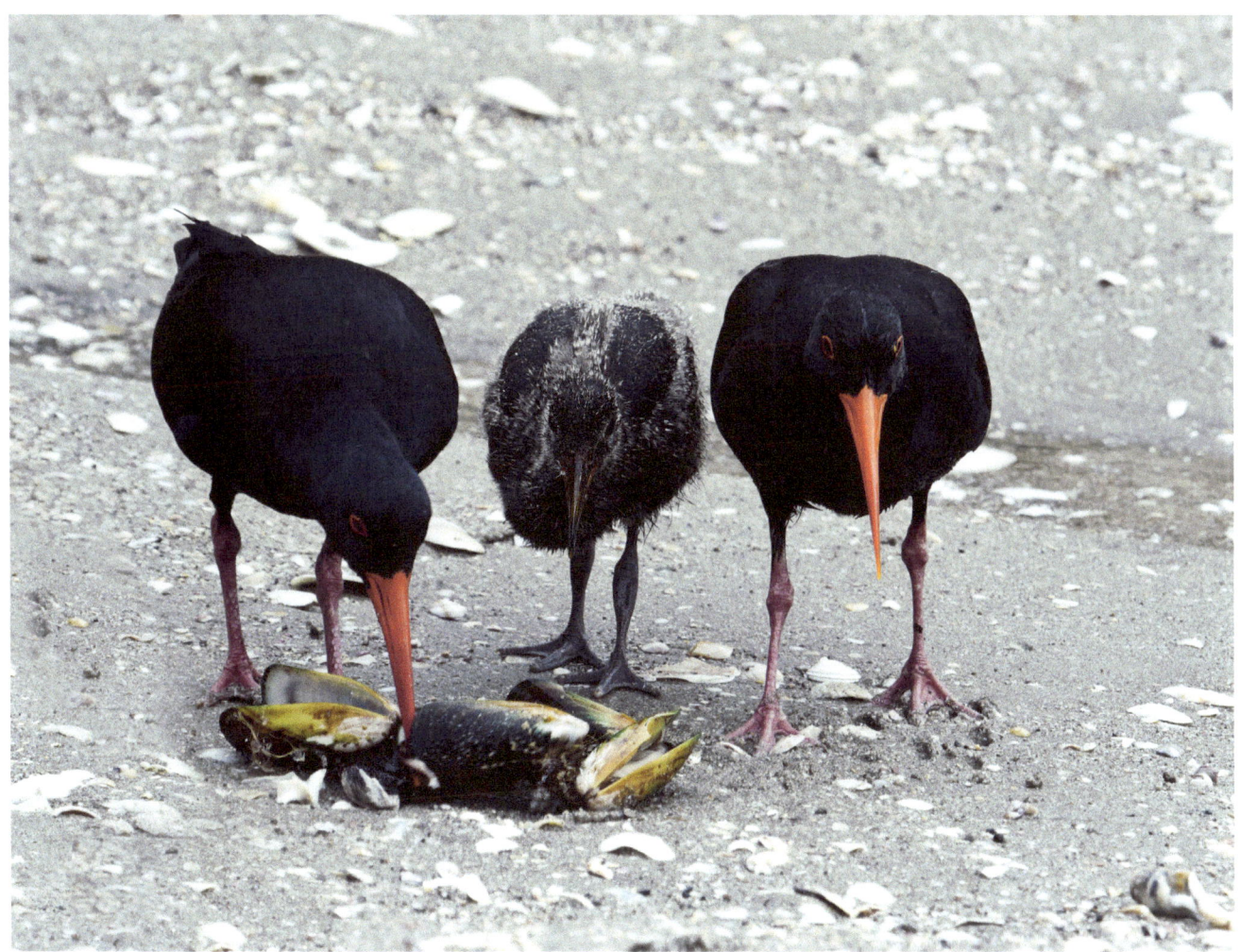

Mussels for breakfast. The bird at the right shows how narrow the bill tip is. These birds probe in the sand as well as getting mussels from the rocks. December.

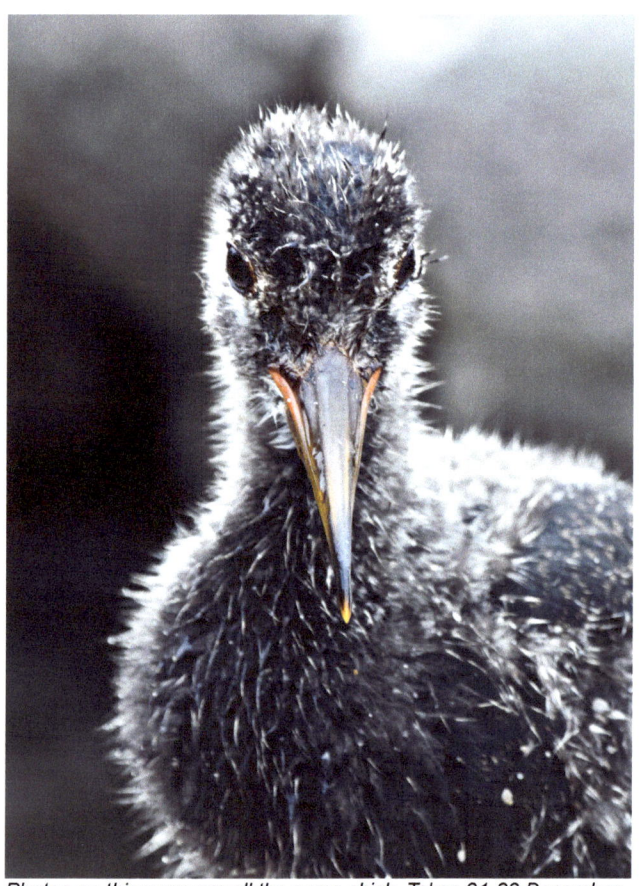

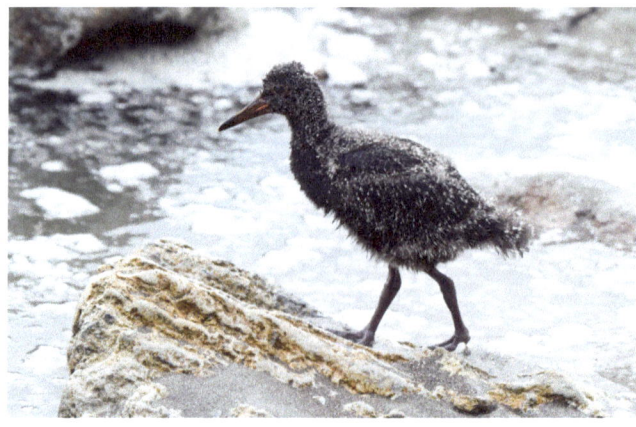

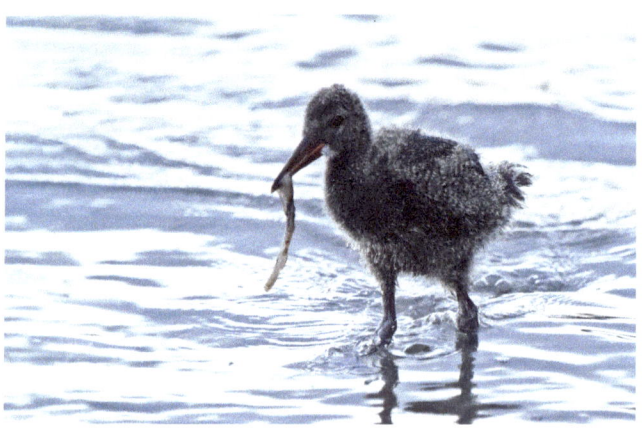

Photos on this page are all the same chick. Taken 21-23 December, it is just starting to fledge so has down with a few feathers.

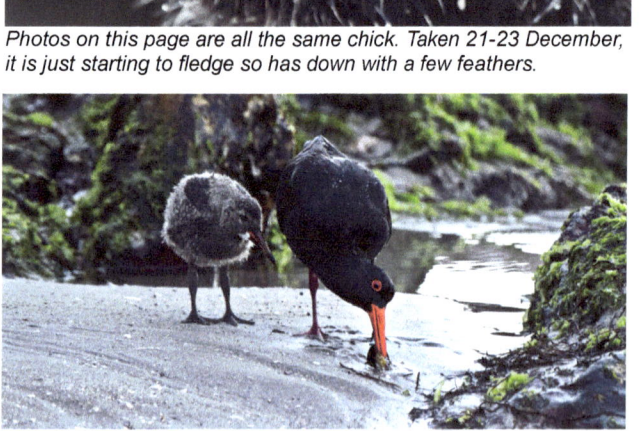

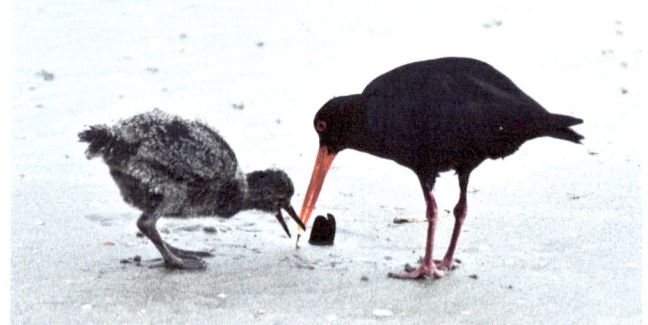

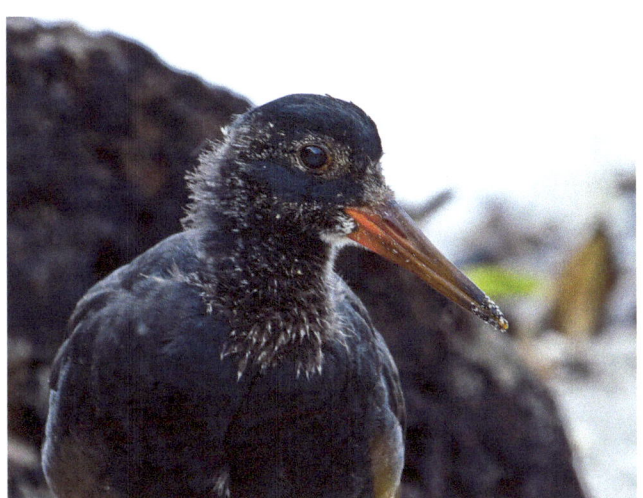

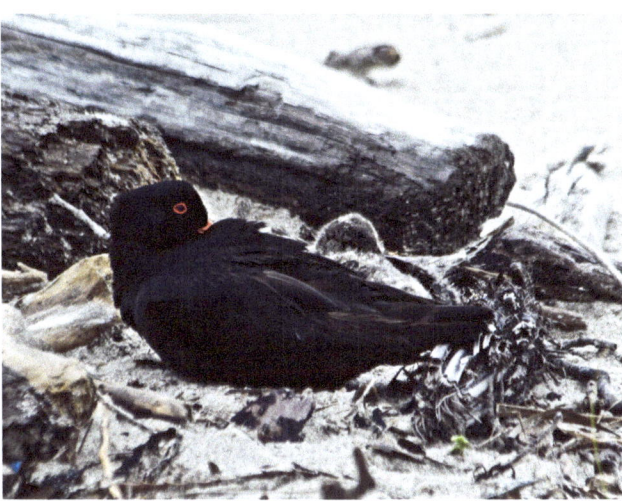

The same bird as the previous page just two weeks later, now showing more feathers. 6 January. Above, below and below right.

Resting together, unconcerned about being watched. January.

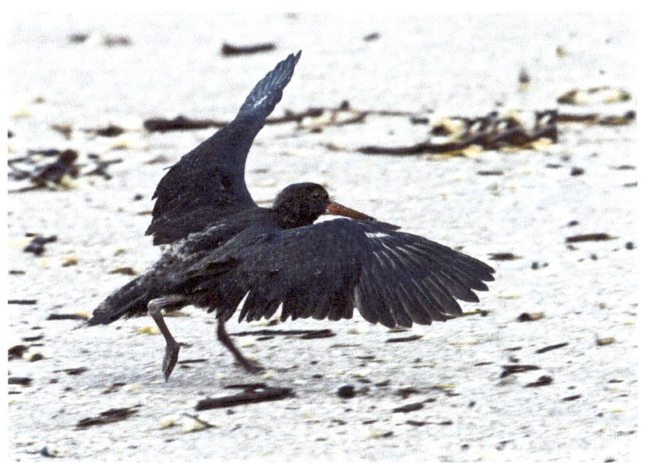

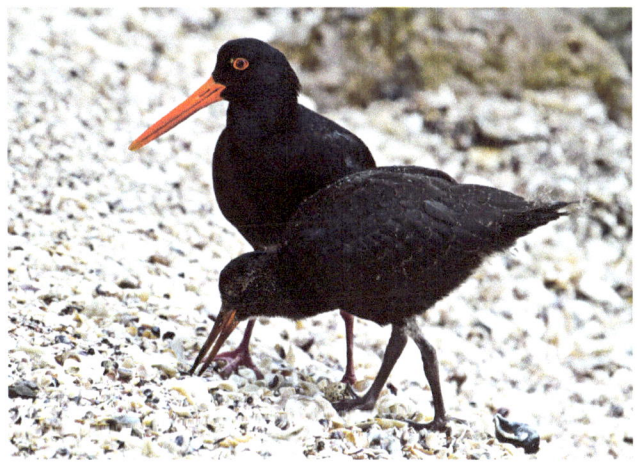

At Pakiri, north of Auckland, there is a sand spit with colonies of NZ dotterels, NZ fairy terns and VOCs sharing the space. The spit is managed for the protection of the endangered birds and is on the far side of the estuary, but of course the birds don't stay behind the fences. In the photos on this page, a VOC chick and its parent were caught on a sand bar by the incoming tide.

Then the most amazing thing happened. The adult bird flew across the channel and waited at the shoreline. The chick entered the water and swam across. It was pushed well upstream by the incoming tide so swam, and eventually ran, far further than the actual distance it needed to cover. On landing on the far side, instead of going straight to its parent, it headed for shelter, presumably its nest site. The parent watched it and when the chick was safely on its way home, it went to the nest site itself. A happy ending for a small baby.

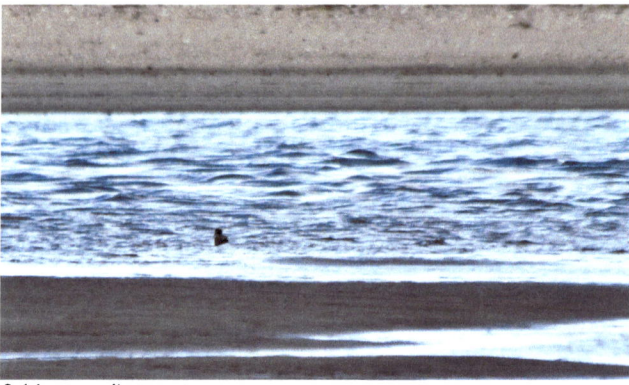

6:14pm, on its way.

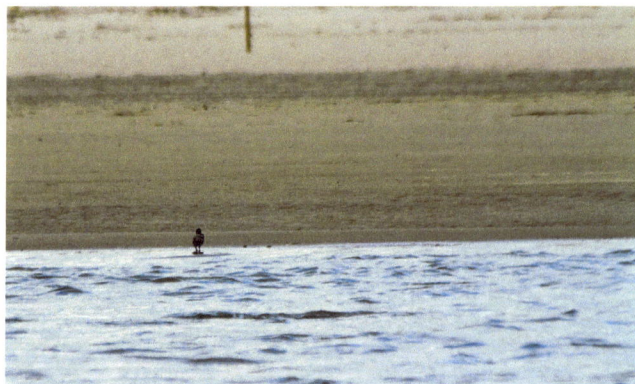

6:16pm, reaching the far shore.

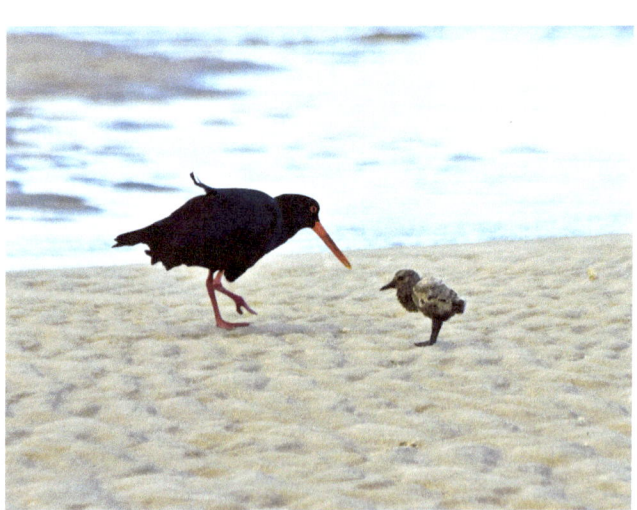

Relaxed before the tide cut them off. All photos this page November.

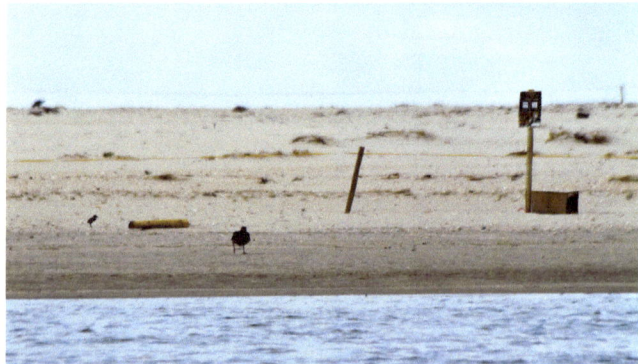

6:18pm – pausing for a rest while heading for safety. The destination was behind the pest trap next to the sign.

Pied morph VOCs are more common in the north and Kapowairua is about as far north as it is possible to go so the birds shown on this page are not unusual from that perspective. What was surprising was that their parents were intermediate morphs that were nearly all black. It is generally believed that young VOCs will be a similar colour to their parents, but these birds seem to be different.

Their territory is the back of the sand dunes, around the edges of the lagoon when it is tidal and also into the camping ground. They also venture onto the sandy shore.

There is a regular flow of fishermen and tourists in this area, but the remote location means that overall there are relatively few people around. These birds are therefore not as comfortable with people as those from well-populated areas, but they do slip through camp itself from time to time when it is quiet.

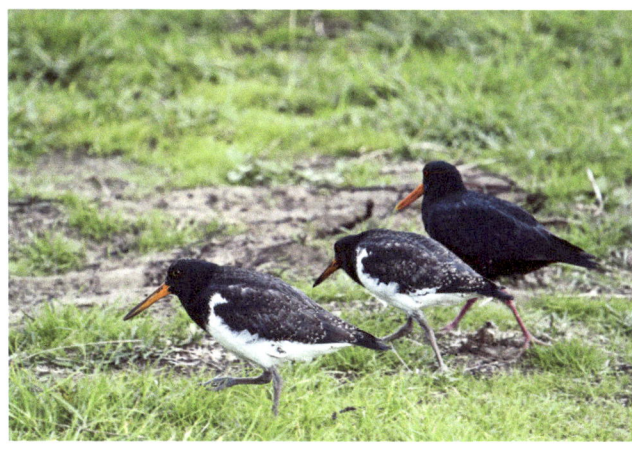

Above and below – a nearly all black pair of intermediate morph VOCs were parents to three pied morph young. All three immature birds were nearly identical, including a white shoulder patch. The parents were likely the same as for the bird shown below left, but without positive identification that can't be certain. April.

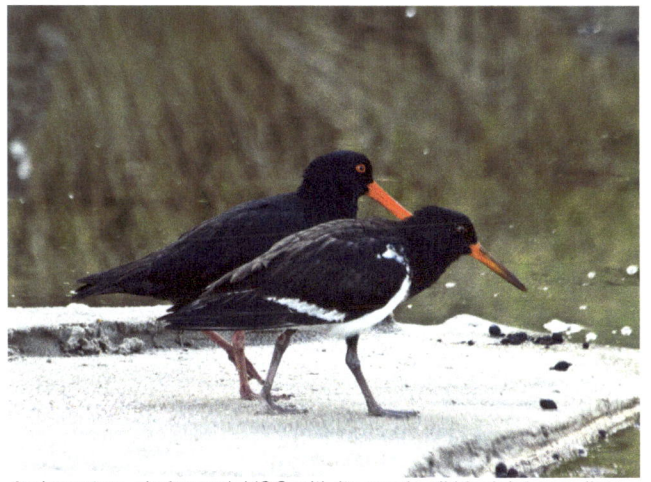

An immature pied morph VOC with its nearly all black intermediate morph parent. This was the season prior to the photos at right. April.

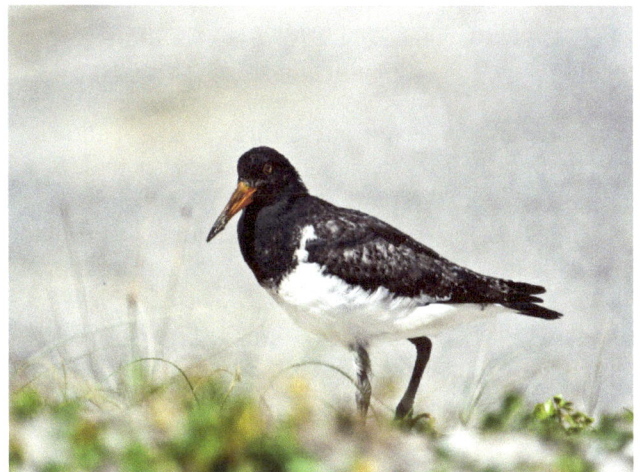

BATHING AND PREENING

Feathers are very important for birds. They keep the bird warm and dry, allow it to fly, and are also used for communication. It is therefore not surprising that birds spend a lot of time caring for their feathers by bathing and preening.

Bathing is done to clean the feathers and birds such as oystercatchers that live in a marine environment will bathe in salt water.

Preening is the bird's way of grooming itself. It checks through all its thousands of feathers; straightening, placing and oiling them. The oil comes from special glands near the tail and the bird uses its bill to distribute the oil along the length of each feather.

During the moult feathers may be shed during preening. The old feathers are replaced by new ones growing through from underneath. These keep the bird fresh and healthy, and are how the birds change colour as they mature and signal readiness for pairing by adopting their breeding plumage.

Watching birds preen is interesting because it allows us an opportunity to see their feathers better and to appreciate the colour and structure of them. After a preening session the bird will often stretch and provide a good view of its wings.

Preening may be seen at any time the bird is relaxed and if done in our presence, it indicates that it is fairly happy about us being there, which is always nice.

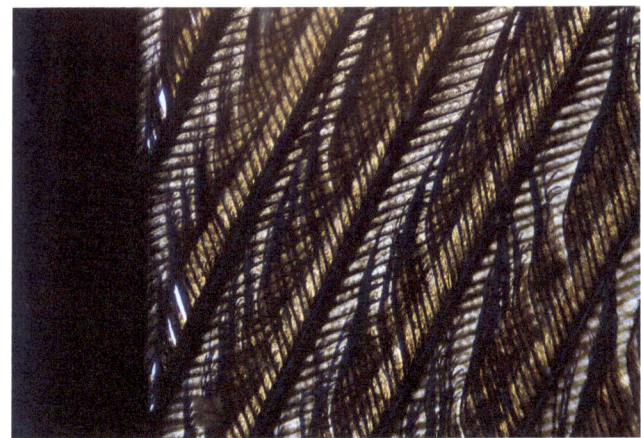

A feather under the microscope. The solid black area to the left is the shaft that runs up the centre of the feather. The dark lines joining the shaft at an angle are the barbs which are what we see with the naked eye. What we need the microscope to see are the barbules that branch from the barbs. They overlap and hook together to prevent air from flowing through which allows the bird to fly. This is a "black" feather from a VOC.

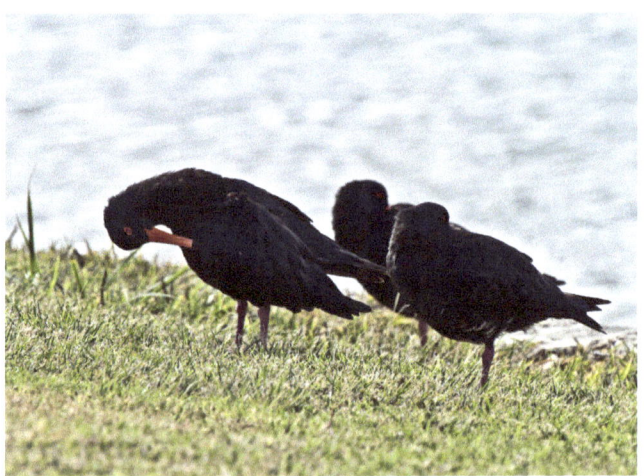

When preening the bird goes through its feathers; cleaning, oiling and straightening them. They must all be properly aligned so that the barbs and barbules are all in place and working well to insulate the bird against cold, to keep it dry and to enable efficient flight. Black morph VOC. Ruakaka, Northland. April.

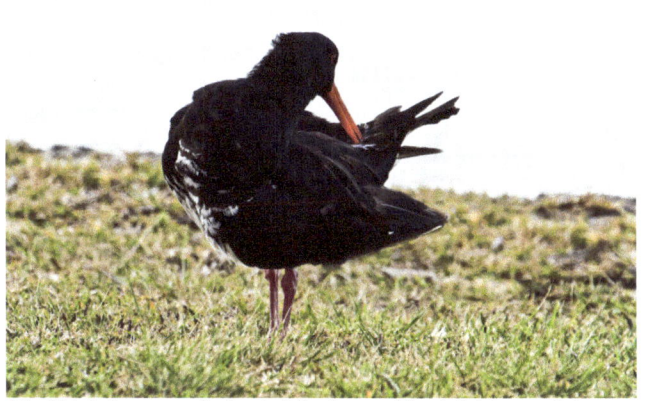

Most birds have an oil gland at the base of the tail. Intermediate morph VOC. Ruakaka, Northland. April.

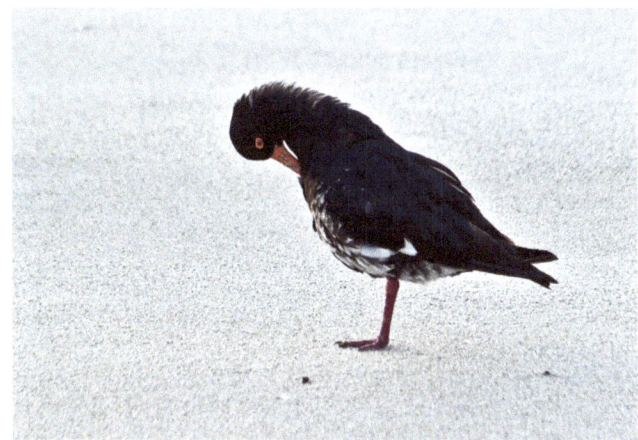

The long bill can be both an asset and a hindrance. Intermediate morph VOC. Pakiri, Auckland. April.

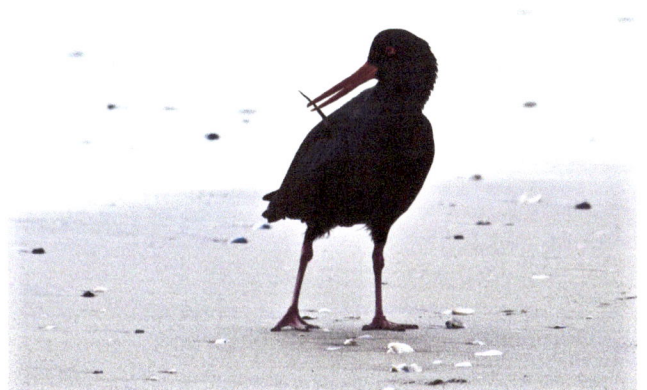

Every last feather must be put into place. Black morph VOC. Mount Maunganui. July.

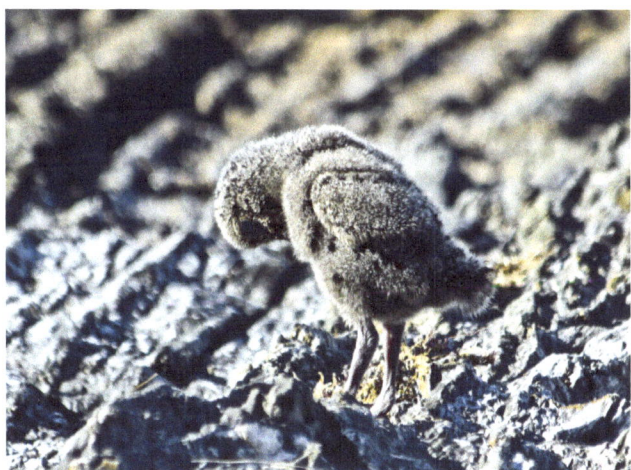

Chicks also need to preen Black morph VOC. Otarawairere, Whakatane. February

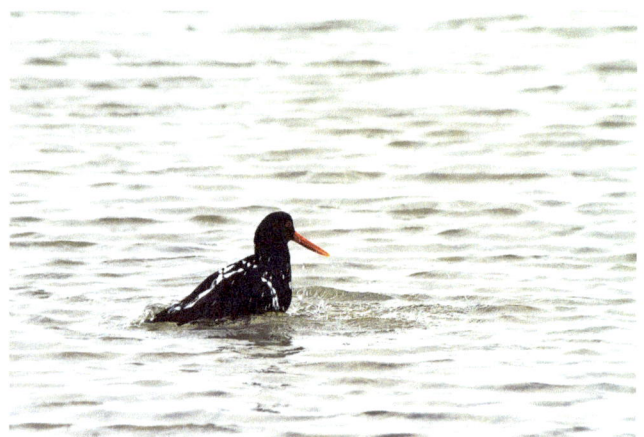

Bathing is also an important part of the care of the feathers. Black morph VOC. Maketu, Bay of Plenty. June.

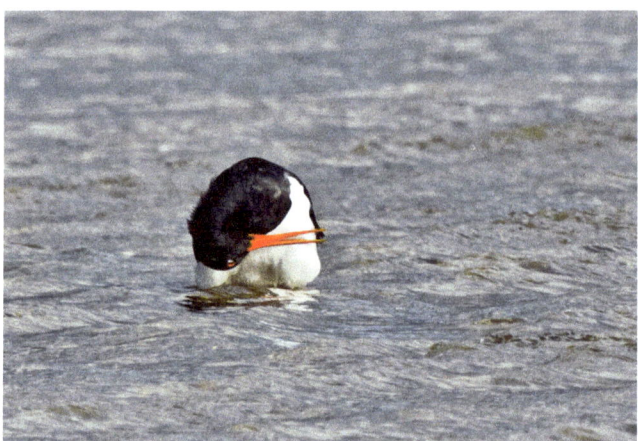

Birds will be seen rubbing with their heads to spread oil among the feathers. SIPO. Ruakaka, Northland. April.

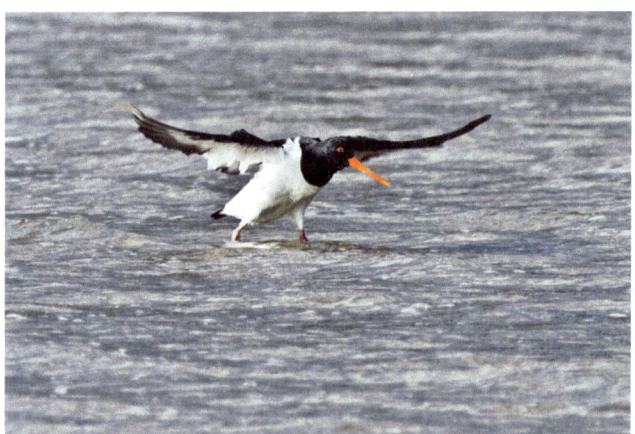

A bathing or preening session will often be completed with wing stretching or beating. SIPO. Ruakaka, Northland. April.

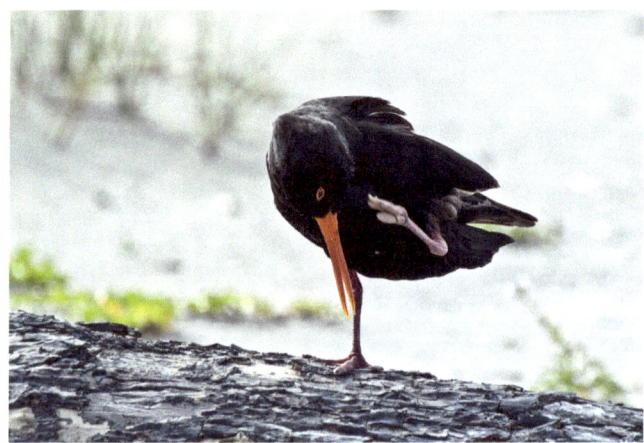

Sometimes a scratch is all that's needed. Black morph VOC. Pukehina, Bay of Plenty. December.

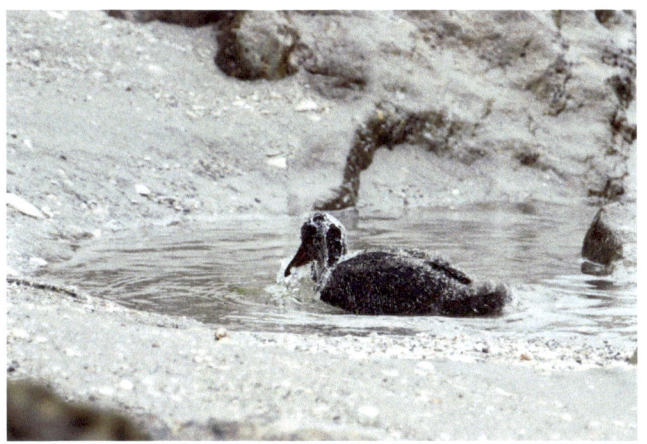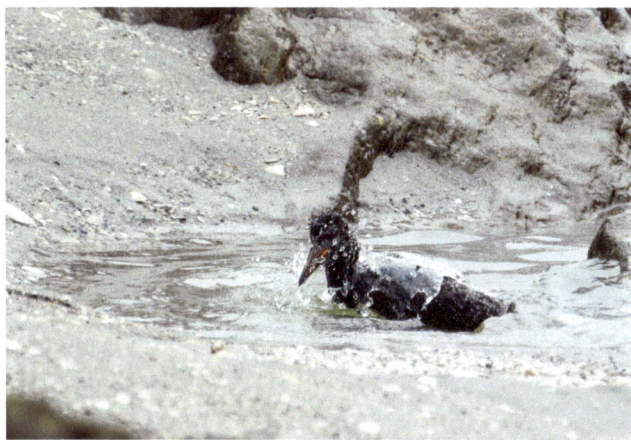

Young birds follow the same bathing routine as adults as shown here. This chick selected a small tide pool and spent a good two minutes bathing before stretching its little wings and going on its way. This page Mount Maunganui. December.

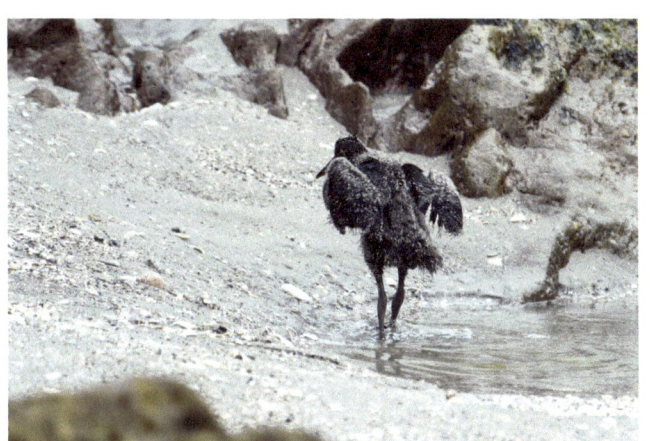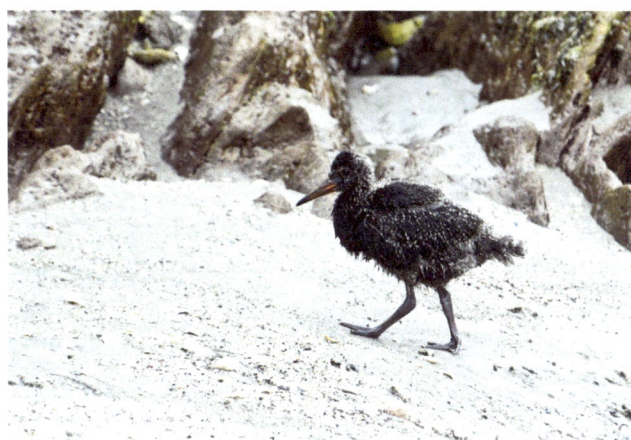

LAST VIEWS

These are a few last photos to show the birds' lives – feeding, flying, roosting. They are always active and are fascinating to watch as they go about their daily lives, working hard to look after themselves and their families.

Whatever they are doing, birds have a great view of the world that we see only from the ground.

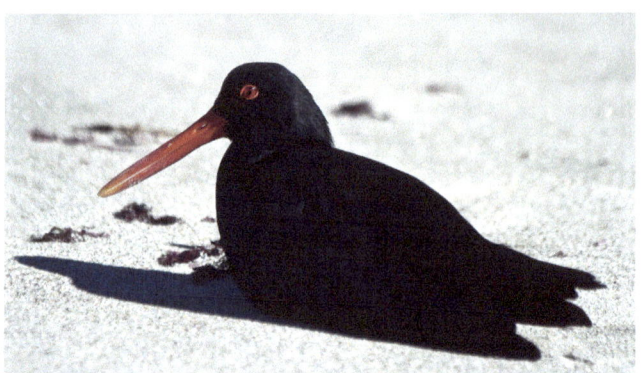

Black morph VOC relaxing in the sun. Mount Maunganui. May.

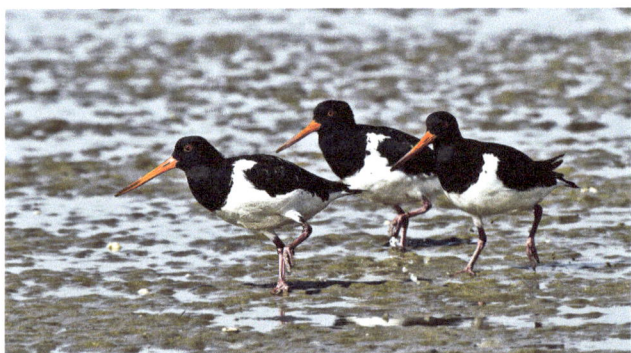

Group of SIPOs. Ruakaka, Northland. April.

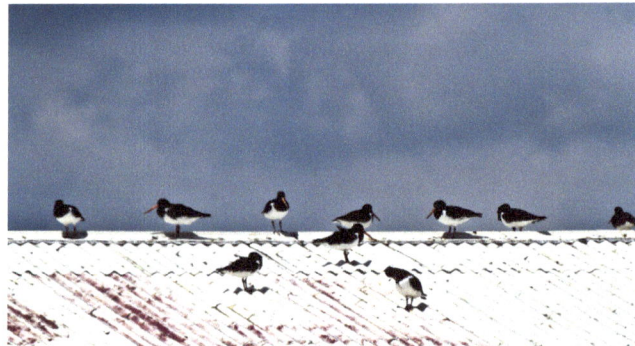

Human activity can encroach on harbour-side roosting areas. These SIPOs have solved the problem by roosting on this roof, the highest in a group of buildings near the estuary. Tauranga. February.

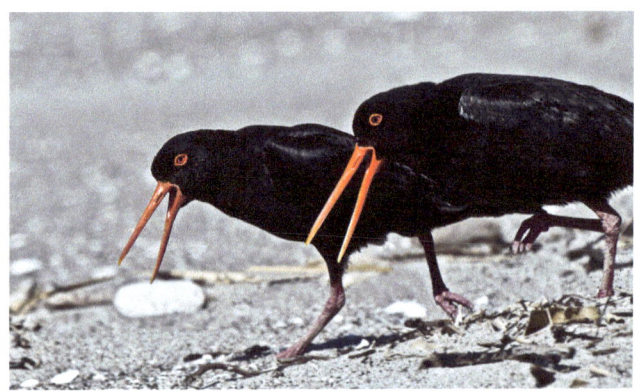

VOCs in a piping display. Pukehina, Bay of Plenty. January.

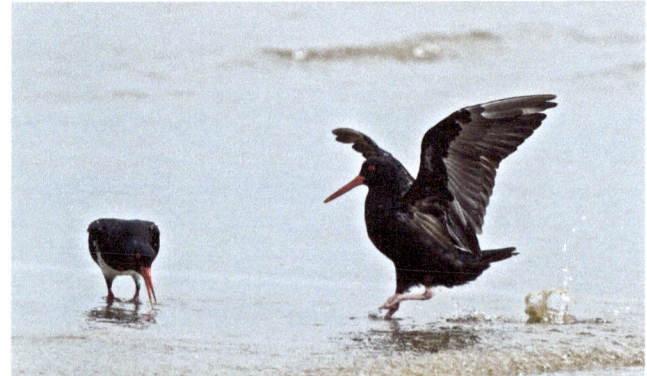

The SIPO at left showed its displeasure that the black morph VOC at right landed so close to it. Tokerau Beach, Northland. April.

42

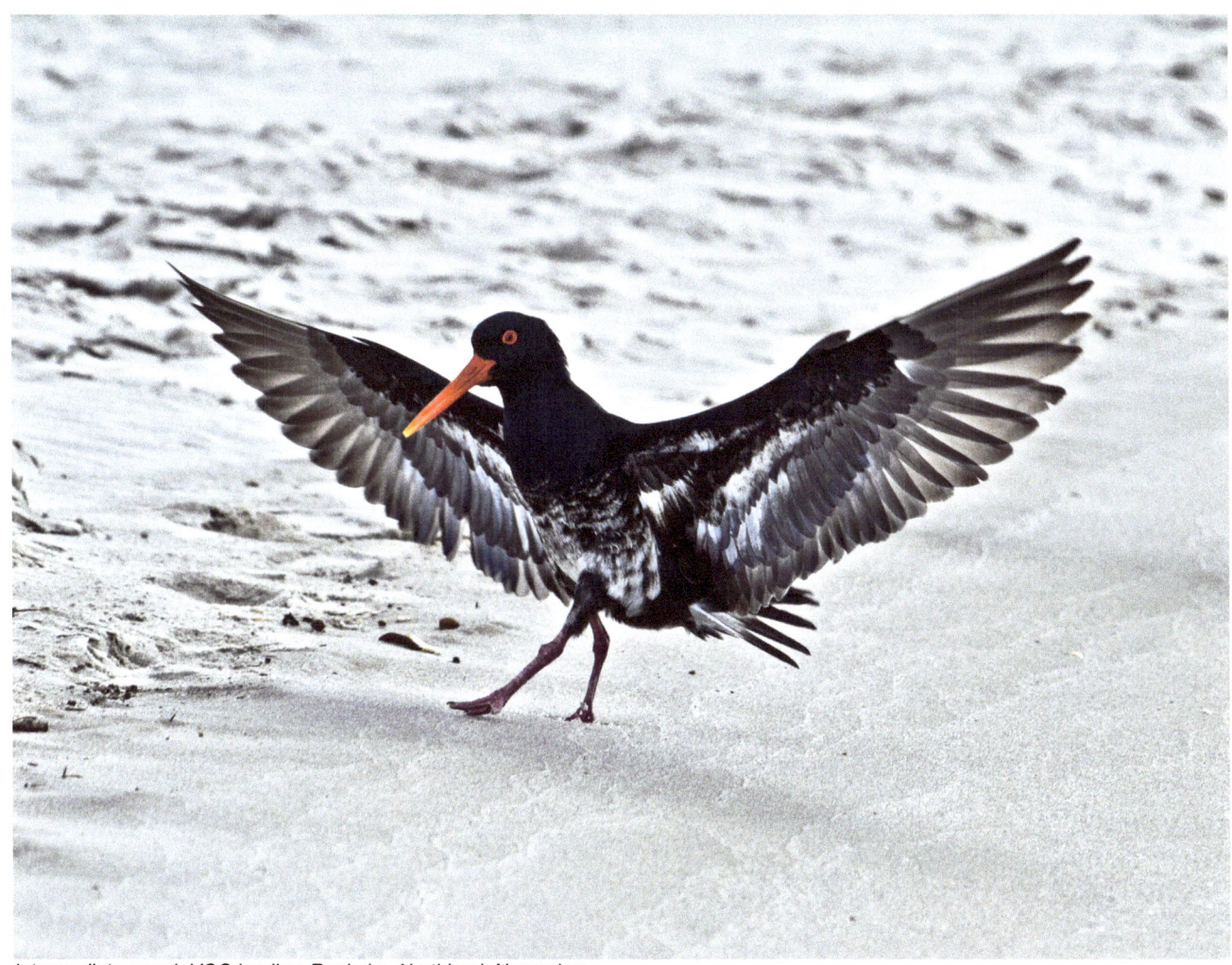

Intermediate morph VOC landing. Ruakaka, Northland. November.

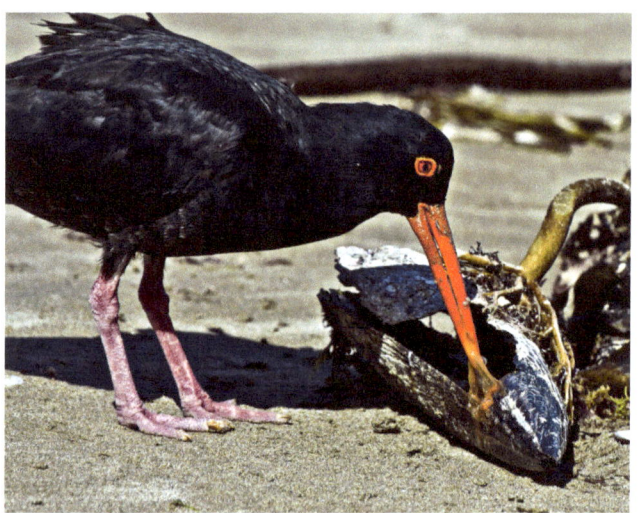

A horse mussel washed up on the beach provides a good easy meal. Black morph VOC. Opito Bay, Coromandel. February.

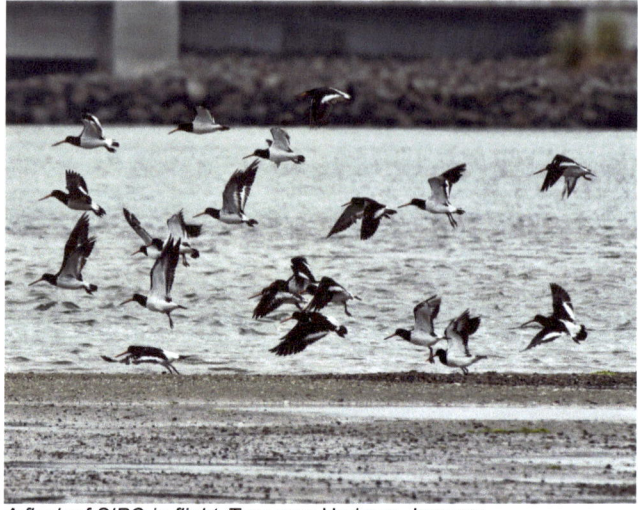

A flock of SIPO in flight. Tauranga Harbour. January.

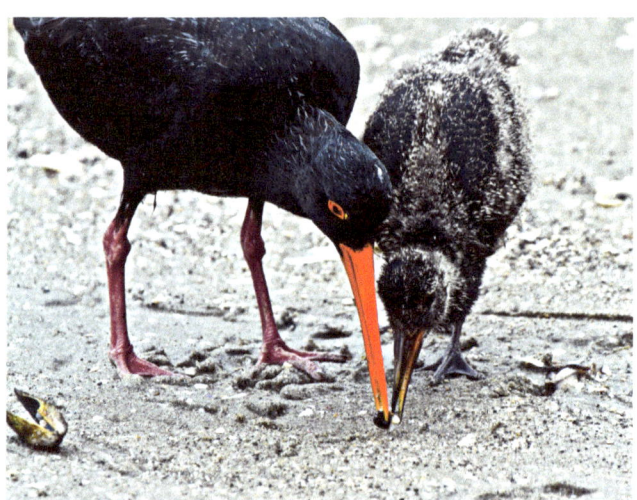

VOC parent and chick feeding together. Mount Maunganui. December.

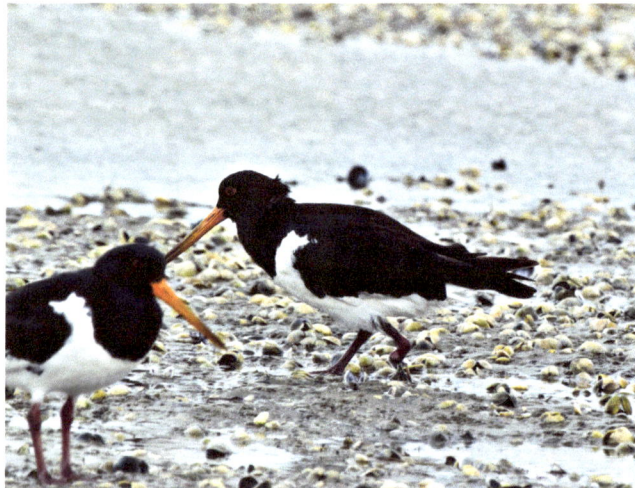

Congenital deformity, injury from fishing line or caused by predators? Birds with missing feet are quite common. This SIPO hobbled around the cockle strewn beach with the rest of the flock. Houhora, Northland. April.

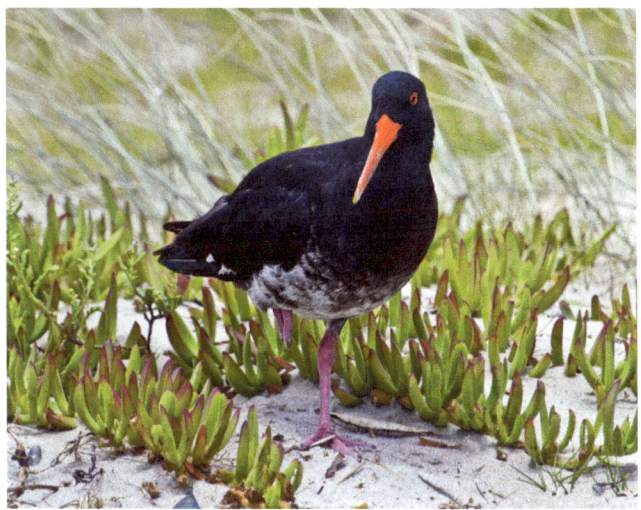

Intermediate morph VOC resting on one leg after foraging in sand. Opito Bay, Coromandel. February.

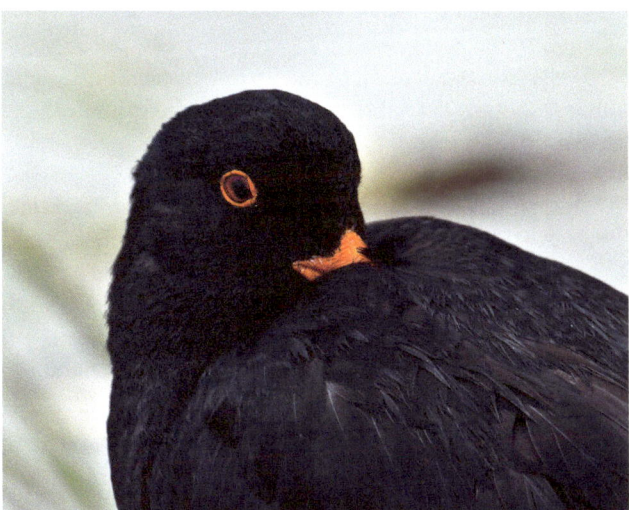

This black morph VOC became so used to me that its efforts to warn its chick of potential danger were no more than a half hearted muffled sound coming occasionally from under its wing. It didn't even bother lifting its head. Mount Maunganui. January.

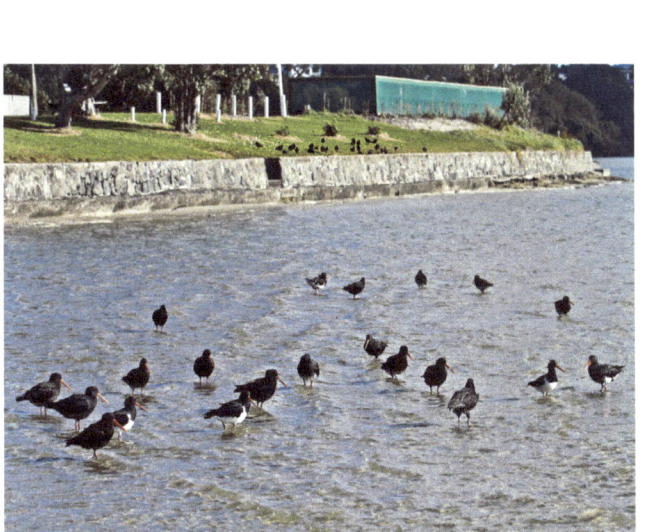

A mixed group of SIPOs and VOCs wading in the shallows at high tide while another group of VOCs roosts on the bank in the background. Ruakaka, Northland. April.

OTHER OYSTERCATCHERS

- **Chatham Islands oystercatcher** *(Haematopus chathamensis)* is the only other oystercatcher found in New Zealand and is found only in the Chatham Islands. It is a pied oystercatcher, similar to the South Island pied oystercatcher but closer to the size of the variable oystercatcher.

Internationally there are a number of other species of oystercatcher but these are not seen in New Zealand at all.

FURTHER INFORMATION

This is a small selection of the variety of books and other resources available to the person who is interested in learning more about these birds.

Arkins, A. & Doel, L. (2005). *Introducing New Zealand birds.* Auckland: Reed.

Baker, A. J. (1972). *Systematics and affinities of New Zealand oystercatchers.* Unpublished doctoral thesis, University of Canterbury, Christchurch, New Zealand. Available online at http://ir.canterbury.ac.nz/handle/10092/6169.

Buller, W. L. (1888). *A history of the birds of New Zealand.* London: Buller. Available online from http://www.nzetc.org/tm/scholarly/tei-BulBird.html.

Chambers. S. (1989). *Birds of New Zealand : locality guide.* Hamilton: Arun.

Chambers, S. (2007). *New Zealand birds : an identification guide.* Auckland: Reed.

Chudleigh, B. (2001). *Shorebirds of New Zealand : a photographic showcase.* Katikati: B. Chudleigh.

Handbook of Australian, New Zealand and Antarctic birds. (Vols 1-7, 1990-2006) . Melbourne: Oxford University Press.

Heather, B. D. & Robertson, H. A. (2005). *The field guide to the birds of New Zealand.* Auckland: Viking.

International Union for Conservation of Nature. *IUCN red list of threatened species.* http://www.iucnredlist.org.

Medway, D. G. (2002). *The Reed field guide to common New Zealand shorebirds.* Auckland: Reed.

Medway, D. G. (2002). S*ea and shore birds of New Zealand.* Auckland: Reed.

Moon, G. (2002). *A photographic guide to birds of New Zealand.* Auckland: New Holland.

Moon, G. (1995). *Common birds in New Zealand 2.* Auckland: Reed.

New Zealand birds : nga manu o Aotearoa http://www.nzbirds.com/.

Royal Forest and Bird Protection Society of New Zealand. http://www.forestandbird.org.nz/.

Ornithological Society of New Zealand http://osnz.org.nz/.

Reader's Digest (1985). *Complete book of New Zealand birds.* Sydney: Reed Methuen.

Robertson, C. J. R., et al. (2007). *Atlas of bird distribution in New Zealand : 1999-2004.* Wellington: Ornithological Society of New Zealand.

Sagar, P. M., Barker, R. J. & Geddes, T. (2002). Survival of breeding Finsch's oystercatchers *(Haematopus finschi)* on farmland in Canterbury, New Zealand. *Notornis, . 49,* 233-240. Available online at http://notornis.osnz.org.nz/survival-breeding-finschs-oystercatchers-haematopus-finschi-farmland-canterbury-new-zealand.

Te Papa, OSNZ & Department of Conservation. *New Zealand birds online* http://www.nzbirdsonline.org.nz/

www.ingramcontent.com/pod-product-compliance
Lightning Source LLC
Chambersburg PA
CBHW041514280526
45792CB00004B/1250